MARKETING ON MAIN STREET

Winning Strategies for

Growing Your Small Business

JOHN T. PETERS

MARKETING ON MAIN STREET

Copyright © 2024 JOHN T. PETERS

All rights reserved.

ISBN: 9798323418039

Is This Book Exclusively for Hackensack, NJ? No.

You'll see that I often refer to Hackensack, NJ, where I'm currently the Executive Director of the Main Street Business Alliance and the Hackensack Performing Arts Center. I love this city, and it's fun to write about. Plus, some awesome businesses are knocking it out of the park regarding marketing and customer service. So, you'll see many of my examples of real Hackensack companies.

However, the information in this book is relevant to any city or town in the USA, from Lubec, Maine, to Coos Bay, Oregon, and from Angle Inlet, Minnesota, to Key West, Florida. So, throughout the book, you'll see "Hackensack (or in any city or town)" listed often. I have done this because I imagine people will skip around, so I want to remind them that the information in this book works almost anywhere.

Be sure to sign up for more information at johntpeters.com.

MARKETING ON MAIN STREET

SPECIAL DEDICATION

To Cathy Panagoulias,

This book is dedicated to you, my dear first cousin, Cathy. Your remarkable journey through life was a beacon of resilience, innovation, and heartfelt support for those lucky enough to have known you.

As a former deputy managing editor at the Wall Street Journal, you navigated the publication through the tumultuous period following the 9/11 terrorist attacks with exemplary leadership and vision. During your influential tenure at the Wall Street Journal, you made significant strides, from directing U.S. news coverage to leading the charge during the early days of the Internet revolution. But beyond the technological advancements, you were instrumental in encouraging managers to prioritize diversity, making an indelible mark on the industry and paving the way for future generations. Since your passing, the hundreds of online comments by former colleagues are a testament to your professional and personal traits and beliefs.

Cathy, our long conversations, filled with insightful learning and shared laughter, will forever hold a special place in my heart. You believed in me and my writing, encouraging me to pursue my passion with the conviction that I had a unique gift. I dedicate this book to you with a mixture of sadness and profound respect. Your encouragement and belief in my abilities have inspired me deeply. This book honors your legacy, incredible life, and the enduring lessons you've shared with our entire big, fat,

Greek Petropouleas family.

With all my love and highest regard,

Your cousin,

Yiannis

(John T. Peters)

For my father, mother, sister, wife, and children.

The Main Street Business Alliance Mission

The Main Street Business Alliance (MSBA) is a public/private partnership formed between the business community on Main Street and the city of Hackensack. The MSBA's mission is to address the issues facing the business community on Main Street, with the goal of improving the local economy and the overall business climate.

The MSBA management organization is governed by a Board of Directors comprised of commercial property owners and business owners who are elected by the members of the district, along with liaisons from the Hackensack Chamber of Commerce and the City Council. The MSBA is supported by a full-time Executive Director. That's me. I serve at the pleasure of the board, which means I report to them, implementing the approved strategic plan.

As such, I wish to thank the members of the Main Street Business Alliance's Board of Trustees for their support.

This includes *Edward Decker, Eric Anderson, Jerry Lombardo, Jason Some, Jose Valencia, Bryan Hekemian, Jay White, Luis Ortiz, Laura Kirsch, Marco Howington, Gary Banoun, William Hanson, Ana Suarez, and Albert Dib.*

I sincerely thank each of you for your critical support, contributions, and guidance. Your collective efforts have been a key factor in the Alliance's successes.

WELCOME INTRODUCTION BY
<u>JOHN T. PETERS</u>

Dear Business Owners and Managers in Hackensack (and beyond!),

Welcome to a journey of growth, learning, and community. I'm John T. Peters, the Executive Director of the Main Street Business Alliance, also called "That Main Street Guy." It's my privilege to guide and support you through the complicated world of marketing your small business on Main Street, whether in Hackensack or any other city or town.

Let me start by telling you about the scariest thing I see on Main Streets across the USA. Picture this: A small business owner wants to open a business on Main Street. They have a passion for operating a business, and they're finally going to do it! They find a location to rent, sign a lease, make a logo, build the store, fill out all the permit applications, and even apply for grants (like the Storefront Façade and Sign grant offered by the Main Street Business Alliance). Some months go by as the cash drains from their checking account. They're at the store every day, making all the improvements to the new store's interior so they can hurry up and open. Initial supplies and inventory are delivered daily, and they've already made friends with the UPS drivers and Amazon delivery guys. Then, opening day comes! They open the front doors…. and…wait. I can't tell you how many small businesses don't have a plan for driving business to their stores or growth plans for their restaurants and cafes. They expect the doors to open and customers to come running in. Unfortunately, it rarely works that way.

My career path includes a blend of entrepreneurial ventures and corporate leadership, providing me with a deep understanding of the challenges and triumphs you face daily.

Since my early days as a serial entrepreneur, starting with Zeus Tours & Yacht Cruises in 1990 (which I sold to FAR&WIDE in 1999), I have experienced the hands-on thrill and challenges of building and selling businesses. (I also know what it's like to worry about making payroll on a Friday.) My journey took me through various landscapes, from international tour operations in Greece to technology startups like Tripology, which I sold to Rand McNally. My corporate tenure has been equally enriching. I have held senior executive roles, like President of USA Today's Travel Media Group, VP of Business Development at RCI/Wyndham, and Managing Director – Mercantile at Brush Creek Ranch, the world's most exclusive ranch resort.

This unique mix of entrepreneurial grit and corporate strategy has taught me the immense value of proper planning, streamlined operations, and effective marketing. I have witnessed firsthand the power of digital and grassroots marketing, understanding that each business has a unique heartbeat and requires a tailored approach. My work, recognized with awards like the GOLD Adrian for Digital Marketing and named "Innovator of the Year" by the US Travel Association, reflects a commitment to innovation and excellence by great, collaborative teams. Do you know what else it represents? Bumps, bruises, and very painful failures.

I bring this experience to the Main Street Business Alliance, where our goal is to empower you, the lifeline of

Hackensack's vibrant community. Where I've succeeded in the past, I'll help you replicate those wins. Where I've failed in the past, I'll help you avoid the same mistakes. The truth is, I understand that running a business is no small task. It demands time, dedication, and a willingness to adapt and grow. Whether refining your marketing strategies, exploring new operational efficiencies, or tapping into the digital world, I am here to assist. But, like you, my team is small. In fact, at the time of this writing, I am a team of one. So, I know where you're coming from on your busiest day.

But, let's acknowledge the work required to be successful. Effective marketing and business management on Main Street requires a hands-on approach, whether you're a cozy café or a bustling retail store. It's about diving deep into the nuances of your business, understanding your audience, and leveraging the right tools and strategies to reach them. This guide is designed to offer you step-by-step insights into making your business thrive.

By the way, I'm from Jersey! At times, I'm going to be blunt.

Remember, I am (we are) here for you, ready to help turn challenges into opportunities for growth. But I should mention one more thing… I'm from Jersey. So, if you ask for help and give me every excuse for why you think something won't work, I will be blunt in my response. Sure, I'll be polite. I'll ask questions to try to understand your hesitation and try again to explain my thought process. I'll help plan out a test so you can try what I'm suggesting. Believe me, I know change is hard. But if you keep giving me excuses, I'll wish you a pleasant day and move on to the next person who wants to think outside the box and at least try to grow their business. After many years I've learned that you can't help someone who doesn't want to be helped.

So, let's embark on this journey with determination and a shared vision for success. Here's to growing, learning, and thriving together on Main Street! If you're not following me on social media, especially on LinkedIn, let's fix that right now. Go to www.linktr.ee/johntpeters and join me on any social media platform you like—or all of them! Be sure to sign up to receive my emails on helpful hints for small businesses.

Warmest regards,

John T. Peters

Executive Director

Main Street Business Alliance

SECTIONS ON AI
ARTIFICIAL INTELLIGENCE

This is Just the Beginning: I've been writing this book for quite some time. Portions of it come from another book I'm writing, all about Strategic Partnerships. In the last year, AI (Artificial Intelligence) and GenAI (Generative Artificial Intelligence) have become monstrous topics. It reminds me of when "the Internet" launched commercially, though I believe it is more significant. If I published this book tomorrow, the AI sections would need updating the day after tomorrow, so I will keep them theoretical versus step-by-step instructions. You'll undoubtedly be reading more from me on AI and GenAI. First, let me give you a quick tip on the difference between AI and GenAI. Traditional AI mainly focuses on data plus a little bit of text. An example would be when a system uses AI to determine when a traffic light turns green. GenAI systems are all about generating completely new text or images on their own, only receiving prompts from the user. As I said, this will change by the second, so check out www.johntpeters.com to get all my updates.

WHAT IS A SPECIAL IMPROVEMENT DISTRICT?

You'll see me refer to Downtown Hackensack, the Special Improvement District I manage as the Executive Director of the Main Street Business Alliance. So, what is a Special Improvement District?

A Special Improvement District (SID), often also known as a Business Improvement District (BID), is a defined area within a city or town where businesses pay an additional assessment or fee (okay, "tax") to fund improvements within the district's boundaries. The primary goal of a SID is to enhance the district's overall vitality, making it more attractive and functional for businesses, residents, and visitors alike.

The concept of a SID is rooted in recognizing that the collective interests of businesses and property owners in a particular area can be better served through cooperation and shared investment. The improvements financed by a SID might include enhanced street cleaning and maintenance, beautification projects like landscaping and lighting, public safety initiatives, marketing, creative placemaking, promotional activities, and hosting special events. These initiatives are typically above and beyond what the city or town usually provides.

The formation of a SID usually starts with a group of business owners or property owners within a specific area who recognize a shared need for additional services or improvements. They may approach the local government with a proposal to establish an SID. The proposal must typically gain approval from most property owners in the proposed district, as they will fund the improvements through additional assessments. The local government then enacts an ordinance establishing the SID.

Once established, a SID is often managed by a board or a nonprofit organization, which can include local business owners and property owners. This management entity decides how the collected funds will be spent within the district. Collaboration between the SID and the local government is crucial, as it ensures that the improvements align with broader city or town plans and regulations.

In short, SIDs are a wonderful asset for any community. If you'd like to learn more about SIDs and BIDs, check out the International Downtown Association (www.downtown.org). If you're in NJ, check out Downtown NJ (www.downtownNJ.com), the only statewide organization focusing on NJ's downtowns. Okay, now that we're all on the same page, let's get started.

TABLE OF CONTENTS

Chapter 1: Understanding Your Market 18

Chapter 2: Branding Your Business 28

Chapter 3: Digital Marketing Essentials for Small Businesses 39

Chapter 4: Local Outreach and Networking 57

Chapter 5: Customer Relationship Management for Small Business 65

CHAPTER 6: ANALYTICS AND MEASURING SUCCESS IN HACKENSACK 74

CHAPTER 7: BUDGETING AND RESOURCE ALLOCATION FOR SMALL BUSINESSES ON MAIN STREET 82

CHAPTER 8: STRATEGIC partnerships AND COLLABORATIONS IN HACKENSACK Building Synergistic Business Relationships 93

Chapter 9: Implementing Future Marketing Trends for Small Business 103

Chapter 10: Grants and Funding Opportunities for Small Businesses 113

Chapter 11: Mastering Offline Marketing in Hackensack . 122

Chapter 12: Engaging Your Community Through Events and Sponsorships 130

Chapter 13: Customer Service Excellence on Main Street 138

Chapter 14: Social Media Marketing in Hackensack's Business Landscape 147

Chapter 15: Mobile Marketing on Main Street USA 157

Chapter 16: Reaching the New Residents 161

Chapter 17: Leveraging AI in Small Business Marketing for Small Business Entrepreneurs 167

Chapter 18: Sustaining Business Growth and Innovation . 177

Chapter 19: Deepening Your Small Business's Community Roots 181

THE FINAL CONCLUSION: 185

EMBRACING YOUR BUSINESS JOURNEY ON MAIN STREET 185

CHECKLISTS 187

RESOURCE DIRECTORY 217

CHAPTER 1:
UNDERSTANDING YOUR MARKET

Chapter Summary and Introduction: Navigating Today's Diverse Market Landscape

If your city or town is like Hackensack, it is vibrant with a unique blend of long-time locals and new residents. In this chapter, we'll explore how to make your business resonate with our diverse community, whether you run a nail salon, a chic boutique, or a buzzing jewelry store.

Let's start with a deep dive into Hackensack's demographics. Our town is a colorful mix of long-time residents and fresh faces, and connecting with them involves more than just selling products. We'll look at creative ways to engage with different groups, like hosting community events or using social media to highlight what makes your business unique. Remember that viral crème brûlée bagel video? If not, you can find it on DowntownHackensack.org) That's the kind of content that gets people talking!

Next, we'll examine the latest local trends and how you can capitalize on them. Whether adding a health-conscious menu to your restaurant or creating a cozy reading corner in your café, staying in tune with today's interests is key. I'll guide you through competitive analysis – a "secret mission" to uncover what makes other businesses successful and how you can do even better.

We'll also discuss how to welcome new residents to town openly. From exclusive deals to special welcome packages, there are great ways to reach out to young professionals moving into new apartments.

By the end of this chapter, you'll have a blueprint for making your business a beloved part of our vibrant community. So, let's dive in and make your business the talk of the town! As a bonus, I've included checklists at the end of the book to help you on your journey.

If you're still reading after all this, that's a good sign. So, welcome, Main Street Entrepreneurs of Hackensack and across the USA! You are the lifeblood of our community, bringing diversity, flavor, and innovation to our streets. To succeed, you must understand the local market – a crucial first step in tailoring your business strategies to today's unique environment. Every city and town has unique characteristics, and Hackensack is no exception.

Understanding the Demographics

Before doing anything, check the demographics of your market. An easy way to do this is by visiting the US Census website at census.gov.

National census data is incredibly helpful for small businesses because it shows how markets change over time. However, it's important to understand the pros and cons of census data.

Pros:

1. **Demographic Insights:** Census data provides detailed demographic information, including age, gender, income, and household makeup. This helps businesses tailor their marketing strategies to effectively target audiences.

2. **Geographical Detail:** The census offers geographical data that helps businesses understand population densities and distribution, guiding decisions on where to focus marketing efforts or open new locations.

3. **Trend Analysis:** Regularly collected census data allows businesses to monitor long-term trends in population growth, demographic changes, and

income shifts. This helps predict future market conditions and make informed decisions.

Cons:

1. **Outdated Data:** Since the census is not conducted annually, the data may not reflect current market conditions, leading to inaccurate assumptions.

2. **Lack of Detail for Niche Markets:** Census data is general and may not provide specific information about niche markets' hobbies, behaviors, or preferences.

3. **Complexity:** The vast amount of data can be overwhelming, making it difficult for those without data analysis experience to extract useful information without significant time or investment.

Balancing the completeness and reliability of national census data with the potential for outdated information and the need for more specific market intelligence is crucial. Small businesses might benefit from combining census data with up-to-date and focused market research, like what the MSBA offers. We're happy to work with you to compile demographic data that makes sense for your business.

Hackensack is a mosaic of cultures and lifestyles, from long-standing residents to young professionals moving into new high-rise apartments. It is vital to recognize the nuances of these groups.

Long-term Residents: These individuals value community, tradition, and personal connections. To appeal to them:

- Host community events or sponsor local sports teams or events.

- Share stories of your business' history and involvement in the community through in-store displays, local advertising, or social media.

- Offer loyalty programs or discounts for regular customers.

New Young Professionals: This tech-savvy group values convenience and new experiences. They often move to places like Hackensack for more affordable rent than their previous locations. I often get asked, "Can you believe they're paying $3,000 a month for rent in that new building?" and my response is always, "Yes, they're saving money because they were paying $5,000 a month for a studio in New York City."

- For restaurants, implement online ordering systems like Grubhub or Uber Eats or develop a mobile app for reservations or retail e-commerce.

- Ensure your business is listed on your Special Improvement District's or Chamber's website and apps. In Hackensack, we have an amazing digital footprint, including our app, developed with Distrx. Visit linktr.ee/hackensack to access all of our links.

- Use social media to showcase trendy aspects of your business, like a clothing store highlighting the latest fashion or a café showing off a stylish interior or new drink. Remember BEC Bagel's crème brûlée bagel video? It got almost 800 views in the first 24 hours!

Analyzing Local Market Trends

Staying attuned to local trends is essential. For example, there's a growing interest in health and wellness nationwide, and Hackensack is no exception.

- A restaurant could introduce a health-conscious menu featuring fresh, local ingredients. Greek Island Grill is a great example, offering dishes perfect for the Mediterranean Diet.

- A clothing store might expand to include activewear.

- Consider hosting events or workshops related to these trends, like a fitness day sponsored by local gyms such as Kaizen Fitness or Femme (a gym in Hackensack exclusively for women).

Conducting a Competitive Analysis

Understanding your competition is crucial. Here's how you can keep your finger on the pulse of what is happening in your town or city:

- **Visit and Observe:** Stroll around your town and nearby towns within a 10-mile radius. Note what similar businesses are doing, how they attract customers, and what promotions they run. Sign up for their emails and follow them on social media.

- **Identify Gaps:** Look for missing services or products. For example, Iconic Coffee installed a privacy booth for customers to work or take calls, and Casamont Tech opened a tech repair shop to fill a local gap.

- **Adapt and Innovate:** If a competitor's marketing strategy is effective, consider ways to adapt and improve it for your business. This could involve borrowing successful ideas from businesses outside your immediate area.

Engaging with New Residents

Hackensack has gone through an amazing transformation over the past eight years, with a dozen new buildings with thousands of new apartment units. For you, as a small business owner, attracting the young professionals who are moving into these new buildings requires strategic outreach.

- Collaborate with apartment complexes to promote exclusive deals for new residents. The easiest way to do this is to work with the MSBA and ensure that your business is listed on our site and app, which are great places to advertise your discounts.

- Include information about your business and a special first-time visit offer in our welcome packages for new residents.

AI Topic: How to Use Artificial Intelligence (AI) for Predictive Analytics

Imagine running a café and wondering how to keep up with customer preferences. AI can be your secret weapon. It goes beyond tracking past sales, diving into trends, social media posts, local events, and even weather changes. For instance, AI might notice that customers crave warm drinks and comfort food on rainy days. With this insight, you can prepare a "Rainy Day Special" featuring hot chocolate and fresh-baked cookies whenever the forecast predicts rain. AI helps you stay a step ahead, turning data into smart decisions. See the resource list at the end of this book for a list of different AI tools.

Case Studies: Hypothetical Business Scenarios

1. **Café Tranquilo:** This local café struggled to attract younger customers. They revamped their menu to include trendy plant-based and gluten-free options. They used Instagram to showcase their new offerings, leading to a noticeable increase in foot traffic from nearby high-rise apartments.

2. **TechTown Gadgets:** This small electronics store recognized a need for tech workshops. They started hosting weekly sessions on smartphone usage and online safety, drawing a steady stream of new and long-standing residents.

Conclusion: Your Market, Your Blueprint

Understanding Hackensack's market, or any market across the USA, involves embracing its diversity, recognizing its needs, and aligning your business strategies accordingly. Whether adapting your services, leveraging local trends, or connecting with new community segments, your journey to business growth starts with this fundamental step.

CHAPTER 2:
BRANDING YOUR BUSINESS

Summary and Introduction: Crafting A Memorable Identity

Welcome, friends, to the next step in your entrepreneurial journey on Main Street - building a strong, recognizable brand. Whether you operate a bustling ethnic restaurant, a sleek mobile phone store, or a trendy clothing boutique, your brand is your story and promise to your customers. Be sure to emphasize the word "promise" in your mind as it comes up a lot in this book.

Main Street, anywhere in the country, can be a dynamic and competitive market, so creating a strong brand identity for your small business is crucial for standing out and resonating with customers. A clear and easy-to-understand brand helps you stand out from the crowd. This chapter provides an in-depth, step-by-step guide to developing your brand identity, designed for those new to the branding concept.

Understanding the Essence of Branding

Branding is more than just a logo or a catchy slogan; it's the emotional and psychological relationship you establish with your customers and the promise of service you offer them. When customers first walk into your establishment, what do they see? Is it clean? Is your staff smiling? It's about emotion and perception and creating an image that sticks in the minds of your customers and aligns with their values and needs.

1. **Defining Your Brand**: Define what your business stands for. What are its core values? Most importantly, what unique experiences or services does it offer? For instance, a family-owned Colombian restaurant might emphasize its authentic cuisine and warm, homely atmosphere.

2. **Identifying Core Values**: List the values important to your business. These could include quality, customer service, innovation, or community involvement.

3. **Creating a Brand Personality**: Think of your brand as a person. Is it friendly and approachable, like a neighborhood café? Or is it sleek and professional,

like a high-tech gadget store? This personality will guide your branding decisions.

4. **Visual Identity**: Your brand's visual identity includes your logo, color scheme, and overall design aesthetic. It should reflect the personality of your business. A tech store might opt for a sleek, modern design, while a boutique might choose a more eclectic, personalized look.

5. **Logo Design**:

    - **Conceptualization**: Start with brainstorming ideas that represent your business. Sketch out ideas or work with a graphic designer. Your goal should be to have different versions of your logo for other uses:

        - **Primary logo**: The main logo used most frequently, including all elements of your brand and text for your company name. Have three versions:

        - **Full color**

        - **One-color**: Useful for one-color flyers.

- **Reverse**: For use over dark backgrounds or photos.
- **Secondary logo**: A stacked version of the primary logo for when space is an issue, typically in full color.
- **Brandmark**: An abstract representation of your brand that can stand alone and is useful for social media profiles.
- **Animated logo**: An animated version for digital platforms. This is a newer trend and can easily be created with online tools. Just search for "create an animated logo" and you'll see a bunch of options.
- **Simplicity and Memorability**: Your logo should be simple enough to be recognizable and memorable. Think about iconic logos and what makes them effective.

6. **Choosing a Color Scheme**:
   - **Color Psychology**: Research how different colors evoke certain emotions. There's plenty of science behind this. For example, green often represents freshness or eco-

friendliness. Here are some other common color associations:

- **Blue**: Trust, reliability, stability
- **Red**: Passion, energy, action
- **Green**: Growth, health, renewability
- **Black**: Elegance, sophistication, strength
- **Gray**: Neutrality, calmness, balance
- **Yellow**: Happiness, optimism, warmth
- **White**: Purity, cleanliness, simplicity
- **Pink**: Femininity, softness, care
- **Orange**: Creativity, enthusiasm, playfulness
- **Purple**: Luxury, royalty, wisdom
- **Brown**: Earthiness, reliability, sustainability
- **Teal**: Serenity, calm
- **Burgundy**: Sophistication, ambition

- **Gold***: Prosperity, wealth

- **Silver***: Modernity, sleekness

- **A special note about metallic colors in your logo**. Be careful when using metallic colors. If you ever must print anything on paper, metallic colors are difficult, or at the least more costly, to create.

- **Consistency Across Branding**: Use your color scheme consistently across all branding materials, including your storefront, website, and marketing materials.

Developing a Strong Brand Message

Your brand message communicates your unique value proposition to your customers. It should be clear, consistent, and targeted.

1. **Crafting Your Message**: What sets your business apart? This is often referred to as your USP (Unique Selling Proposition). For a service provider like a phone store, it might be exceptional customer service or cutting-edge products. Ensure this message is reflected in all your communications.

2. **Consistency Across Channels**: To build recognition and trust, maintain consistency in your brand message across all platforms—from your storefront to your website and social media. Ensure your message is coherent whether a customer reads a flyer, browses your website, or visits your store.

Implementing Your Brand Across Customer Touchpoints

Your brand should be consistently represented at every customer touchpoint.

1. **In-Store Branding**:

    - **Store Layout and Design**: Ensure your store's interior design reflects your brand identity. This includes the use of colors, signage, and the overall layout. Keeping a clean, tidy store is critical. By the way, if you serve food, your bathrooms better be modern and spotless.

    - **Employee Uniforms and Behavior**: If you have uniforms, they should align with your brand colors and style. Train your employees to embody your brand values in their interactions with customers. At the very least, they should be smiling, friendly, polite and approachable.

2. **Online Branding**:

   - **Website**: Your website should mirror your brand's visual and messaging elements. Ensure it is user-friendly and offers a seamless brand experience. Remember, the easier and more enjoyable a customer's journey is to buy from you, the more likely they will.

   - **Social Media**: Use consistent branding across your social media platforms. This includes using your brand colors, logo, and voice in your posts. Also, make sure you proofread your posts. Spelling errors are amateurish and unprofessional.

Evolving and Refreshing Your Brand

As your business and the market evolve, so too should your brand.

1. **Conduct Brand Audits**: This is a fancy way of saying you should review your brand periodically to

ensure it aligns with your business goals and customer expectations. Survey friends, family, and customers' opinions on your logo drafts. Trust me, other people will see things you don't.

2. **Refreshing Your Brand**: If needed, update your brand. This could be a logo refresh, an update to your color scheme, or a new tagline. Ensure any changes are still aligned with your core values and business objectives.

Engaging Your Audience with Your Brand

1. **Telling Your Story**: People connect with stories. Share yours through social media, in-store displays, or community events. Maybe your clothing store started with a small sewing machine in your living room, or your restaurant recipes have been passed down through generations.

2. **Community Involvement**: To reinforce your brand presence, participate in or sponsor local events. For instance, a clothing store could host a local fashion show, or a restaurant could cater community events.

Leveraging Local Culture in Your Branding

Cultural diversity is an asset in so many cities across the USA, especially Hackensack. Wherever your business is located, embracing local themes, traditions, or trends in your branding is a good idea to create a deeper connection with the community.

1. **Cultural Celebrations**: Participate in cultural festivals or host events celebrating Hackensack's diversity. This will help your brand stand out and show how much you value the community.

2. **Local Collaborations**: Partner with other local businesses or artists to create unique, Hackensack-centric products or experiences.

Using AI-Driven Brand Analysis and Development

Let's say you're the proud owner of a local boutique. You're thinking, "How do I make my brand pop?" This is where AI steps in, almost like a branding guru. It looks at everything from the colors you use on your website to the language in your ads. AI even monitors your competitors, giving you insights like, "Hey, your competitor's eco-friendly angle resonates with customers. Maybe highlight your green practices?" AI can also track customer responses to your marketing campaigns, telling you what's working and what's not. It's like having a 24/7 focus group, giving you the lowdown on your brand's strengths and areas for growth.

Case Studies: Hypothetical Success Stories

1. **'Sabor de Hackensack'**: This local Dominican restaurant used vibrant colors and traditional motifs in its branding, which appealed to the city's Latino community. They hosted weekly cultural nights that became a local hit, reinforcing their brand as a cultural hub.

2. **'Urban Style Collective'**: A small boutique collaborated with local artists to create Hackensack-inspired clothing lines. Their brand became synonymous with local art and style, attracting a diverse clientele.

Conclusion: Your Brand, Your Signature

No matter where your business is located, your brand is your handshake, story, and promise (there's that word again!) to your customers. It's also the customer service experience when someone enters your establishment. It's a blend of who you are, what you offer, and how you connect with the community. As you build and refine your brand, remember that it's an ongoing journey of aligning your business's identity with the needs and aspirations of your customers. Let your brand be a beacon on Main Street, inviting, engaging, and memorable.

If you come away with anything from this chapter about doing business on Main Street, it should be that people buy from people, not stores, and they buy what they like and need.

CHAPTER 3:
DIGITAL MARKETING ESSENTIALS FOR SMALL BUSINESSES

Summary and Introduction: Embracing the Digital Revolution

If you own a small business, you'll regularly find yourself delving into the exciting world of digital marketing!

This chapter is your go-to guide for boosting your small business's online presence, tailored specifically for today's vibrant business scenes. Consider this your friendly roadmap to navigating the digital landscape, packed with practical tips and relatable examples.

We'll start with the basics: why every business, even yours, needs a website. It's your online storefront, so make it inviting and easy to navigate! We'll also cover local SEO tricks to help customers find you and how to get those valuable customer reviews without feeling awkward about it.

Next, we dive into content marketing – the art of telling your story online. Whether it's blogging about industry trends or showcasing your products on Instagram, we've got you covered. Social media isn't just for puppy videos; it's a powerful tool for connecting with customers. We'll explore which platforms are best for your business and how to engage your followers.

We'll also demystify social media influencers. Even small businesses can benefit from influencer partnerships, *if* you choose wisely. And finally, we'll tackle email marketing. Yes, it's still relevant, and we'll show you how to keep your customers in the loop without spamming them.

By the end of this chapter, you'll be ready to conquer the digital world and bring your unique business flavor to the online community. This book is my playbook for what I'm working on for the Main Street Business Alliance, so let's get your business buzzing online!

1. Building a Robust Online Presence

Your online presence is like the entrance to your digital storefront. It must be inviting and easy to navigate, just like your brick-and-mortar store.

Creating a User-Friendly Website

I can't tell you how many times I walk into a small business with opportunities for our organization to promote them in the press, in email campaigns, and more. More often than I would like, I'm told "We don't have a website…" followed by ridiculous reasons like it's too complicated to build a website, or their business doesn't need a website because everyone knows them. By the way, often, the most common complaint from these businesses is that 'business is slow.' Folks, a website, even a basic one, is crucial to your success. It's simply not optional. Think of it as the foundation of your digital marketing strategy. Now, your website doesn't have to be complicated – just visually appealing, easy to navigate, and informative. For a restaurant, this means having menus on the site, links to an online reservation system, and links to popular delivery platforms. For a retail store, detailed product listings and an e-commerce platform. The back of this book contains lists of resources, but I'll give you a quick tip; building an online site is easy. With some basic tech skills, you could build one yourself. Programs and platforms like WordPress, GoDaddy, Wix, and others are easy to use and very cost-effective. My preferred one is WordPress. I have built a dozen sites in the last few years using WordPress. Plus, they even offer hosting services and plugins for just about anything, like social media widgets that connect website users to your social media links, newsletter signup widgets, and thousands more. Honestly, setting up an online store is just as easy, if not easier. Platforms like Shopify make setting up an e-commerce site a breeze. And, if you want to create a customized merch (merchandise) store, filled with promotional items like t-shirts, hats, mugs, etc. WITHOUT having to actually buy inventory, you have dozens of platforms from which to choose. So, in about ten minutes, you could have a custom store with items branded with your logo, all available for sale, complete with credit card processing. Check out Printify, Printful, and others. Just search for "online merch store."

Now, let's say you want to build a website or create a merch store but cannot do it alone. You're busy—I get it—so why not hire someone? Go over to Fiverr and create a free account. Then, search for the service you're looking for, say, website creation. Fiverr will connect you with professionals who offer these services. You pick a couple from the list and contact them for a quote. Within no time, you'll be connected and hiring someone. Keep in mind that many of the service providers are located other countries, like India. I've used Fiverr many times, and I'm always impressed with the quality of work I receive from the service professionals who use Fiverr to find new clients.

Website Design Basics

Layout and Navigation: Design a clean layout with easy navigation. Include clear headings and a menu with links to different pages (e.g., Home, Menu, Products, Contact).

Content Creation: Write engaging content that accurately represents your business. Include your business history, product descriptions, and contact information. Remember, a content strategy is important.

Visual Elements: Add high-quality images or videos of your products or services. Ensure these visuals are professional and reflect your brand identity.

Mobile Responsiveness: Ensure your website is mobile-friendly, as many customers browse on their phones.

Basic Search Engine Optimization (SEO)

Properly implemented SEO will improve your website's visibility on Google and other search engines. It does this by making it easier for potential new customers to find your website in the first place so they can find you.

Understanding SEO

SEO is the process (I say 'art') of optimizing your website to rank higher in search engine results. The key to success is using relevant keywords, creating quality content, and ensuring your website offers a user-friendly customer journey and purchasing experience.

Keyword Research

Use tools like Google Keyword Planner to find relevant keywords for your business. For example, a café in Hackensack might target keywords like "best coffee in Hackensack" or "Hackensack café."

On-Page SEO

Incorporate these keywords naturally into your website's content, titles, and meta descriptions. Ensure each page has a unique title and description.

Optimizing for Local SEO

What good is a website if no one can find it? Small businesses in Hackensack and other cities across the USA often thrive on local customers. Use local SEO strategies to appear in search results when nearby customers are looking for your services. For an effective local SEO strategy, you must include local keywords, register on Google My Business, and encourage customer reviews.

Speaking of Reviews!

Most customers will leave a review if you ask them. It's that simple. Make it easy and timely for them to do so. Several tools are available that simplify this process. Just ask your customers: "If you were happy with your meal (or service), we'd appreciate a review. It only takes a minute and is very helpful." Then, provide a QR code for them to scan.

2. Content Marketing: Telling Your Story Online

Content marketing establishes your brand's voice and authority in your industry. This content should appear on your website and social media accounts.

Blog Posts and Articles

Share stories about your business, industry insights, or tips that resonate with your customers. A mobile phone store could blog about the latest tech trends, a clothing store could post fashion tips, and a Greek restaurant could discuss the benefits of the Mediterranean diet.

Visual Content

Utilize platforms like Instagram and Pinterest to showcase visually appealing content. For a restaurant, this could be mouth-watering photos of dishes; for a boutique, images of the latest fashion line. Remember, people want to see the whole experience – not just the food but also the people, the atmosphere, and the joy of dining at your place.

3. Leveraging Social Media for Engagement

Social media is where conversations happen. It's a tool for building relationships with your customers, not just for promotion. I have written an entire chapter on social media. See Chapter 14.

4. Email Marketing: Direct Connection with Customers

Email marketing remains a powerful tool for personal and direct customer communication. Tools like Constant Contact and MailChimp can help you get started.

Building an Email List

Offer incentives for customers to sign up for your mailing list, such as discounts or free items.

Crafting Effective Newsletters

Keep your audience informed about new products, special offers, and events. Personalize your emails to increase engagement. A monthly newsletter is a great place to start.

Using GenAI Systems in Personalized Digital Marketing

Imagine you run a flower shop with a diverse customer base. How do you make sure each customer sees something that catches their eye? AI steps in to help. It segments your audience based on behaviors and preferences, ensuring personalized marketing experiences. AI tools like Lavender.ai can help you write and evaluate your marketing emails, providing feedback to improve your campaigns.

4. Online Advertising: Reach a Wider Audience

Online advertising can most definitely boost your visibility and assist in attracting more customers.

Social Media Ads

Platforms like Instagram and Facebook offer advertising options to target specific demographics. Be sure to create ads that highlight your special offers or your business's unique aspects.

Google Ads

Consider using Google Ads for targeted advertising based on search queries. This is particularly effective for reaching customers who are actively searching for your products or services.

5. Managing and Updating Your Online Presence

An up-to-date online presence is key to maintaining credibility and customer interest.

Regular Updates

Keep your website and social media profiles updated with the latest information about your products, services, and business hours.

Monitoring Online Reviews

Pay attention to online reviews on platforms like Google My Business and Yelp. Respond to reviews, both positive and negative, professionally and courteously.

AI Topic: Leveraging AI and GenAI to Amplify Your Online Presence

In today's fast-paced world, AI can help you dramatically with your online presence. AI is not just a buzzword but a practical tool that can significantly enhance digital efforts. From sprucing up your website, writing relevant content your visitors will engage with, optimizing everything for search engines, and engaging with your community on social media, AI and GenAI have a role in everything you do online. Here's how AI can transform your digital presence:

AI-Driven Website Enhancement

Creating a website that's both attractive and functional is crucial. Nearly every website-building software now offers personalized web design tools, suggesting layouts likely to engage visitors based on your business type. These AI-powered web builders can automatically adjust your site's design to suit your brand's style and optimize it for desktop and mobile viewing. I like WordPress. Within WordPress, you can use Divi AI, which is a suite of WordPress AI tools. Divi can help you write copy, generate images, and overall improve your website.

AI Chatbots

Did you know you can now easily add AI chatbots to your website? That's right, you can install AI chatbots that will field visitor questions and offer them instant assistance. They can answer common questions, guide users through your site, or even assist with bookings and purchases. Then, you can focus your human staff on the more complicated questions. This improves user experience and frees up your time to focus on other aspects of your business. Salesforce.com now has some AI-powered chatbots that deliver personalized service to their users, and they're built right into the Salesforce.com workflow.

Regarding small businesses, one compelling use case for AI chatbots is in online retail. A small retailer could integrate a ChatGPT chatbot into their e-commerce platform to provide personalized shopping assistance, product recommendations, and even support with order tracking or returns, essentially offering the same in-store experience online. This not only enhances the shopping experience but also builds customer loyalty. Another example is within the service industry. Say Casual Habana, a local Cuban favorite restaurant, or even Nail Boutique, one of the many nail salons, wants to streamline reservations or appointments so they could add a chatbot to their site to help manage reservations or appointments. Specifically, a tool like Google's Business Messages can facilitate these interactions, enabling customers to book, cancel, or inquire about services directly through the chatbot. This efficiency improves customer satisfaction and optimizes the business's operations. To many, using AI seems so far off into the future, but I assure you it isn't.

Smart SEO with AI

SEO – search engine optimization - might seem complicated and daunting, but AI can simplify it. AI-powered tools can analyze your website content and recommend improvements to enhance visibility on search engines. They can help identify the best keywords tailored to your local audience and suggest content topics likely to attract more visitors. Guess what else AI can do concerning SEO? It can analyze the SEO strategies of your competitors, see what's working, and suggest similar changes to your website!

AI tools can also track your website's performance in real time, offering insights into how visitors interact with your site and suggesting changes to improve engagement and conversion rates.

Here are just some of the tools that I know of. There are more popping up every day.

SEMRush: I use SEMRush Writing Assistant, an AI-powered tool that integrates with the various content creation platforms I use to offer real-time SEO recommendations. Real-time! Imagine getting SEO-friendly suggestions as you write content. It evaluates content based on SEO best practices, readability, tone of voice, and originality, and while you're typing, it's providing actionable feedback. Come on. You have to admit this is amazing.

Yoast: The Yoast SEO WordPress plugin is my go-to tool. I use the paid version for everything I write for the websites I manage. It distinguishes itself with a user-friendly interface and an amazing list of features designed to aid in producing SEO-optimized content. I'll write something, and Yoast will tell me what's wrong with it and how it can be improved to boost website visibility online. It uses AI to provide real-time content analysis and then offers AI-driven feedback. It also utilizes AI to refine my keywords, helping identify additional keywords or a different strategy. This one? A must.

MarketMuse: MarketMuse uses AI to analyze content compared to the top-performing content in search engine results for specific keywords. Okay, so don't they all do that? Yes, but MarketMuse provides the standard recommendations for topics and keywords and tells you what questions to cover in your content. Initial reviews are encouraging, so check back for more on this one.

Clearscope: I've started testing Clearscope, which says it uses AI to offer content optimization recommendations; get this based on real-time search engine data. As I understand it, it helps writers and marketers understand which terms and topics are most relevant to their target audience. Done properly, this guides the creation of content that is more likely to rank highly in search results. Keep checking my website for more updates. This is one to watch.

Ahrefs' Content Explorer: I only knew Ahrefs for its backlink analysis, but Ahrefs' Content Explorer leverages AI to discover content opportunities based on topics, popularity, and performance metrics. This is pretty cool. It helps businesses identify trending topics and content gaps within their niche, enabling them to create content likely to attract traffic and earn backlinks. Of course, there are several other ways to find out what questions people are asking –go to Google, and it will show you the questions. Seriously, start there.

The message, in the end, when it comes to SEO and AI, these two are a match made in heaven. By harnessing these AI tools that I mentioned (or the other thousand that will come out when I publish this book), small businesses can drastically improve their SEO strategies, from keyword research and content creation to on-page optimization and competitive analysis. When I'm asked by small business owners who do their content writing where they should start using AI, I always say it should be done with SEO tasks. This is because using AI in SEO saves time and provides a competitive edge by offering data-driven insights that human analysis might miss.

AI in Online Advertising

Regarding online advertising, AI can optimize your ad spend by targeting your ideal audience. By analyzing user behavior and preferences data, AI can help create highly targeted ads, improve ROI, and ensure your advertising budget is used efficiently. But here's the thing. I ALWAYS outsource my online advertising and all the related tracking. To do it properly, you have to know the tools and have the right amount of consistent time to put into it so you're not wasting money.

Embracing AI for Growth

Incorporating AI into your strategy for building an online presence doesn't have to be intimidating. Even with a basic understanding, leveraging these tools can significantly improve how you connect with customers, market your business, and manage your digital footprint. As you continue cultivating your digital garden in Hackensack, consider AI a powerful ally that can help your business thrive in the digital age.

I know the whole AI concept seems complicated right now. Still, by integrating AI thoughtfully into your "online presence" strategy, you're not just keeping up with the digital curve but setting your business apart in our vibrant community. Let AI take some of the heavy lifting off your shoulders, giving you more time to focus on what you do best—running your business.

Case Studies: Hypothetical Digital Success in Hackensack

- **Hackensack's Home Cuisine:** This local restaurant used targeted Facebook ads to reach new customers, offering special discounts to first-time visitors. This resulted in a noticeable increase in reservations.

- **Tech Haven:** A tech store in Hackensack boosted its online sales by optimizing its website for mobile users and implementing a successful email marketing strategy highlighting exclusive deals.

Conclusion: Your Digital Path Forward

In Hackensack's bustling market, digital marketing is not just a trend; it's a necessity. Implement these strategies to connect, engage, and convert your online audience into loyal customers. Embrace the digital realm enthusiastically, and watch as it transforms your business. Remember, people buy from people, not just businesses, so make your digital presence personal and engaging.

CHAPTER 4: LOCAL OUTREACH AND NETWORKING

Summary and Introduction: Fostering Community Connections

This chapter is like your friendly neighborhood block party – it's all about getting out there, meeting people, and becoming a real part of the community. This isn't just about selling stuff; it's about creating relationships that turn your business into a local favorite.

First, we discuss why being more than just a shop on the corner is super important. Maybe you're the restaurant everyone talks about or the store that sponsors the local soccer team. It's all about making your business a friendly face in the crowd.

Then, we dive into making the most of local events. Hackensack has many of these; they're golden opportunities to show off what you're all about. Whether you're throwing your event or joining in on events like Hackensacktoberfest or any street fair in your city, it's your chance to mingle and jingle!

But hey, why stop there? Teaming up with other businesses is like joining neighbors to throw the best yard sale. You'll discover how to pick the perfect partner and create promos that get everyone talking.

Local media—think newspapers, radio, and community bulletin boards—are your neighborhood's megaphone. We'll discuss getting your business in the local spotlight without breaking the bank.

Finally, networking isn't just a fancy buzzword; it's about building a web of contacts to open new doors for your business. We're talking about shaking hands with other business owners, joining groups, and maybe learning a thing or two at a workshop.

So, our goal with this chapter is to help you get your business woven into the city's social fabric, where every smile, every handshake, and every community moment turns your business into a local legend. Let's make your business the heart of the neighborhood!

1. The Value of Community Engagement

Understanding the importance of being not just a business but a member of the community is key.

- **Community Involvement:** This can range from participating in local events to supporting community causes. For example, a restaurant could cater a local charity event, or a retail store could sponsor a youth sports team.

- **Building Brand Awareness Locally:** Community activities increase visibility and create a positive brand association. They show you're invested in business success and the community's well-being.

2. Making the Most of Local Events

Hackensack is home to various local events that offer businesses opportunities to engage with the community. The Main Street Business Alliance, the City of Hackensack, the Johnson Public Library, and many other organizations hold local events. You can always check the MSBA event listing pages at Hackensack Events, or if you're outside of Hackensack, you can check the Chamber of Commerce and local municipal events.

- **Participating in Local Events:** Attend street fairs, festivals, and markets. For instance, a clothing boutique could set up a pop-up shop at a local festival to showcase its latest collection.

- **Hosting Your Events:** Create events that reflect your business's personality and connect with your audience. For example, a tech store could host a tech awareness day, educating the community about online safety or new tech trends.

3. Strategic Collaborations with Other Businesses

Collaborations can open up new avenues for marketing and customer reach. Use the power of partnering with another business to grow YOUR business. For this section, I'm calling a 'collaboration' something like a quick joint event or a one-off promo the companies do together.

- **Identifying Potential Partners:** Look for businesses that complement yours. For example, a phone store could collaborate with a local café to create a 'browse and sip' experience.

- **Joint Promotions:** Work together on promotions or events that benefit all involved parties. This could include cross-promotions, joint loyalty programs, or co-hosted events.

4. Utilizing Local Media

Even though we now live in a very digital world, some old, tried-and-true methods still work, so you should consider including them in your mix. Local newspapers, blogs, and community podcasts are good ways to reach the Hackensack community.

- **Press Releases and Local Advertising:** Share news about your business, like a new product launch or an upcoming event, with local media outlets. The Main Street Business Alliance would happily help you promote your business as part of our PR campaign.

- **Community Features:** Get involved in community stories or segments. A restaurant owner could be featured in a local food blog, or a clothing store's fashion tips could be included in a community magazine.

5. Networking for Business Growth

Building a strong network with other business owners and professionals in Hackensack can lead to new opportunities and insights.

- **Business Networking Groups, Workshops, and Seminars:** Participate in the Main Street Business Alliance's Meetups to connect with other local entrepreneurs. Think about it – it's completely worth your time if you develop one successful idea or meet one potential collaborator at just one event. You should also strongly consider joining the Chamber of Commerce for the same reason: small investment and big potential return.

Case Studies: Success Through Community Engagement

- **'Café Cultura':** This local café saw a significant increase in customers after participating in and sponsoring community cultural events, highlighting their commitment to celebrating Hackensack's diversity.
- **'Urban Gear':** A sporting goods store in Hackensack collaborated with local gyms and fitness instructors to host community fitness events,

broadening their customer base and establishing themselves as a hub for local fitness enthusiasts.

Using AI to Best Take Advantage of Local Events

The role of AI in leveraging local events for small business growth can be very significant. AI can deeply analyze community engagement patterns and preferences, allowing businesses to identify the most impactful events for their specific audience. For example, let's say you're a boutique clothing store on Main Street. You could use AI to track fashion-related activities in the community and align its participation or sponsorship accordingly. AI can also personalize marketing strategies for these events, ensuring promotional content reaches the right audience at the right time and maximizing engagement and attendance. Post-event, AI's ability to analyze customer feedback and social media engagement provides valuable insights, helping businesses refine their approach for future events. This comprehensive, data-driven strategy, powered by AI, enhances a business's presence at local events and strengthens its connection with the community, driving growth and brand loyalty.

Conclusion: Weaving into Hackensack's Social Fabric

Local outreach and networking are about more than just business growth; they're about becoming vital to the Hackensack community. By actively participating in and contributing to the community, your business becomes a recognized and respected name, laying the foundation for long-term success and growth. Remember, every handshake, every community event, every smile when a customer walks into your business, and every collaboration weaves your business deeper into the vibrant social fabric of Hackensack.

CHAPTER 5: CUSTOMER RELATIONSHIP MANAGEMENT FOR SMALL BUSINESS

Summary and Introduction: Cultivating Lasting Customer Relationships

This chapter is all about CRM – Customer Relationship Management – and it's a game-changer for small businesses everywhere. Those personal connections keep customers returning, whether you're jazzing up nails, showcasing the latest bling, or fitting someone in the trendiest outfits.

First things first, we break down the nuts and bolts of CRM. It's not just a fancy acronym; it's about knowing your customers like the back of your hand and keeping them happy every step of the way. It's all in the details, from remembering their names to understanding what tickles their fancy.

Now, let's talk about your customer database. It's your CRM's backbone –where you keep all those little nuggets of information about your customers. It's like a treasure trove that helps you understand and serve them better.

Then, we spice things up with personalization. Have you ever got a birthday discount from your favorite store? That's personalization in action, and it makes customers feel super special. We'll show you how to segment your customers and tailor your communication to make them say, "Wow, they get me!"

Loyalty programs are next on the menu. These aren't just about collecting points; they're your secret sauce for customers returning for more. We'll walk you through creating a loyalty program that's simple yet irresistible.

But what about all the data you've collected? That's where CRM tools strut in. These tools are like your business's crystal ball, helping you make smart decisions based on what your customers love and need.

And remember, while chasing new customers is great, your current customers are your gold mine. They're easier to sell to, cost less to keep, and can be your biggest fans, spreading the word about how awesome you are. We'll remind you why focusing on them can boost your bottom line.

So, buckle up and prepare to make every customer feel like the MVP. With CRM, you're not just running a business;

you're creating a community of fans who can't wait to return. Let's turn your customers into your biggest cheerleaders!

1. Understanding the Fundamentals of CRM

Good CRM practices allow you to create and maintain an enthusiastic customer relationship. It's a systematic approach to managing customer interactions and data throughout the customer lifecycle.

- **Why CRM is Crucial:** In a city like Hackensack, where personal connections and community feel matter, CRM can differentiate between a one-time transaction and a lifelong customer.

- **Components of CRM:** CRM incorporates collecting customer data, tracking interactions, and analyzing the customer's actions and overall behavior to personalize communication.

2. Building a Robust Customer Database

Okay, stop right here. This is critical. Really. You need to understand your customer database is the foundation of effective CRM. It should capture relevant information that can be used to understand and better serve your clientele. It would be best if you were tracking who your customers are, what they buy from you when they buy from you, their zip codes, phone numbers, emails, social media accounts, etc. I always ask small businesses about their knowledge of their customer base. I start with one simple question: "Can you produce a list of your top ten customers for the last six months, how much they've spent, and their contact information?"

- **Data Collection Techniques:** Implement methods to collect customer information, like loyalty sign-ups or during purchase processes. For a restaurant, this could be gathering emails for a booking system; for a retail store, it could be during checkout.

- **Maintaining Customer Privacy:** Ensure you're transparent about collecting and using customer data, adhering to privacy laws, and building trust with your customers. This is not to be overlooked and will be a topic of discussion at one of our meetups.

3. Enhancing the Customer Experience through Personalization

Personalization is key to making customers feel valued. Tailor your interactions based on the data collected to enhance their experience. Would you rather get an email that says "Dear Customer" or "Dear Fran"?

- **Segmentation:** Segment your customers based on criteria like purchase history, preferences, or demographics. For example, send targeted email promotions to customers based on their previous purchases.

- **Tailored Communication and Offers:** Use the data to send personalized offers and birthday discounts or invite them to events that align with their interests.

4. Implementing Effective Loyalty Programs

Loyalty programs encourage repeat business and foster a deeper connection with your customers.

- **Designing a Loyalty Program:** Create a program that rewards customers for repeat purchases. This could be a points system, discounts on future purchases, or exclusive offers. It doesn't need to be complicated. A simple program is better than a complicated one. You could even have a simple punch card for every purchase.

- **Promoting Your Program:** Ensure your customers are aware of and excited about your loyalty program. Promote it through in-store signage, social media, and at the point of sale.

5. Utilizing CRM Tools for Analytics and Insights

It would be best if you made serious efforts to use various CRM tools to analyze your customer data, especially to go deep and discover what their behavior means. This way, you can make informed decisions to expand your product lines and services and, most importantly, to improve your services.

- **Choosing the Right CRM Tool:** Select a CRM tool that suits your business's size and nature. Tools like HubSpot or Salesforce offer various features that can be tailored to your needs.

- **Making Data-Driven Decisions:** Remember, the data is your friend (even if you don't like what it tells you). So, use the insights from your CRM efforts and tools to change your marketing strategy and, most importantly, enhance customer service and product lines.

But no matter your growth plans, don't forget your existing customers.

I'm a big fan of focusing on your existing customers before you start any major growth plans. Why? New customers cost more to acquire, so you are reducing costs by focusing on existing customers. Existing customers are also easier to sell to. They already know and trust you. Finally, existing customers can be your biggest cheerleaders. Who better to tell people how great you are than your existing customers? So, your immediate goal is to get your existing customers to become regular repeat customers. Why? Repeat customers spend more. The more customers you keep, the more profitable you'll be.

Using AI to Build Customer Loyalty

Here, AI can elevate customer loyalty programs to new heights. Let's say you own a coffee shop. AI can track purchase patterns and customer preferences, suggesting tailored rewards. For example, a customer who frequently orders lattes might receive a 'Latte Lover's Reward.' AI can even predict when customers might be due for a visit, prompting a friendly reminder or a special offer right when they're thinking of a coffee break. It's personalization that not only rewards loyalty but also makes each customer feel special.

Case Studies: Hypothetical CRM Success Stories in Hackensack

- **'Bistro Locale'**: A local restaurant used its CRM system to track customer preferences and dietary restrictions. Personalizing the dining experience significantly increased repeat patronage and customer satisfaction.

- **'TechTown Gadgets'**: This tech store implemented a CRM strategy that included follow-up emails after purchases with personalized tech tips and exclusive offers, leading to increased customer loyalty and upselling opportunities.

Conclusion: The Heart of Hackensack's Business Success

In Hackensack, where every customer counts, effective CRM is not just a strategy but a business philosophy. It's about recognizing that each customer interaction is an opportunity to deepen a relationship, make someone feel valued, and contribute positively to the community tapestry. Embrace CRM as a core part of your business, and watch as it transforms not just your customer relationships but your business as a whole.

CHAPTER 6:
ANALYTICS AND MEASURING SUCCESS IN HACKENSACK

Summary and Introduction: Navigating the World of Business Analytics

In this chapter, we're diving into the core of business analytics. Think of it as discovering valuable insights that can elevate your business, whether you're in the food industry, fashion, or tech repairs.

First, we'll explore why analytics is so crucial. It's more than counting sales; it's about understanding your customers, what draws them in, keeps them loyal, and might drive them away. We'll review key metrics, from foot traffic to website clicks, and introduce you to tools like Google Analytics and social media insights. These tools are essential for any business with an online presence, helping you understand your customers deeply.

Next, we'll show you how to interpret and turn this data into strategic decisions. For example, if your coffee shop is busier on weekends but slow on Mondays, maybe a special Monday promotion could help. We'll also discuss getting to know your customers' habits and preferences, which is crucial for targeted marketing.

While diving into data might seem overwhelming, we'll provide straightforward strategies to help you focus on what's important. We'll end with success stories from Hackensack businesses that have used analytics to improve their operations, from menu changes in a restaurant to effective social media strategies in a boutique.

Join me as we unlock the power of data together. With these insights, you won't just run your business; you'll steer it towards success with confidence and precision!

1. The Importance of Analytics in Business

Analytics offers a clear picture of your business performance, helping you understand what works and doesn't.

- **Why Analytics Matter:** Analytics helps you make informed decisions, optimize operations, and enhance customer experiences. It's about seeing beyond the numbers to understand trends and patterns.

- **Key Metrics to Track:** Focus on essential metrics such as sales trends, customer foot traffic, website visits, and social media engagement. Regularly tracking these metrics over time helps identify patterns and areas for improvement.

2. Setting Up Analytics Tools

Various tools are available to track and analyze your business data, from simple spreadsheets to advanced software.

- **Google Analytics for Your Website:** Gather data using Google Analytics. It tracks website traffic, visitor behavior, and conversion rates, which is crucial for online businesses like clothing stores or restaurants with online ordering.

- **Social Media Insights:** Utilize analytics from platforms like Facebook, Instagram, and Twitter to measure your marketing campaigns' engagement and effectiveness.

3. Interpreting Data and Making Data-Driven Decisions

Data is only as useful as your ability to understand it. Learn how to interpret analytics and turn data into actionable insights.

- **Reading and Understanding Reports:** Break down how to read analytics reports and understand what the data tells you. For example, consider special weekend promotions if online orders spike on weekends. If Mondays are slow, offer Monday specials.

- **Applying Insights to Business Strategy:** Use data insights to make informed decisions about marketing strategies, inventory management, and customer service improvements.

4. Utilizing Analytics for Customer Insights

Understanding your customers is key to tailoring your offerings and enhancing their experiences.

- **Tracking Customer Behavior:** Monitor and meet the needs of your customers, especially in industries like food service, retail, and tech repairs. Start by keeping structured records of customer purchases and preferences, even with simple spreadsheets.

- **Customize Marketing Efforts:** Use data to develop targeted marketing campaigns. Offer first-time purchase discounts or referral bonuses to attract new customers and special deals or loyalty rewards to retain regulars.

- **Proactively Collect Feedback:** Establish a method for getting feedback, such as informal conversations at the point of sale or direct surveys via email. Ask about their preferences and areas for improvement.

- **Analyze and Adapt:** Regularly examine data and feedback to observe trends. Make informed decisions, such as adjusting service offerings, opening hours, or inventory.

- **Boost Customer Satisfaction:** Use insights to improve the customer experience. Add popular items to your menu or stock more of a favored product style. Personal touches, like remembering regulars' usual orders or acknowledging feedback, can greatly enhance customer satisfaction.

- **Segmentation for Targeted Marketing:** Avoid a one-size-fits-all approach. Use customer data to segment your audience and create more effective marketing campaigns.

5. Overcoming Challenges with Analytics

While analytics can be incredibly beneficial, it can also be overwhelming. Here are some tips to help you manage it effectively.

- **Dealing with Data Overload:** Instead of getting lost in too much data, focus on key metrics relevant to your business goals.

- **Keeping Data Organized and Accessible:** Implement best practices for organizing and storing data for easy access and analysis.

6. Analytics in Action: Real-World Examples from Hackensack

- **'Culinary Delights'**: A local restaurant used analytics to discover their most popular dishes, optimized their menu, reduced food waste, and increased profits.

- **'Fashion Corner'**: A boutique used social media analytics to understand which posts drove the most engagement, refined their social media strategy, and attracted more customers.

Using AI for Business Analytics

AI can streamline the analysis of sales trends, customer foot traffic, and online interactions, providing deeper insights into business performance and customer preferences. For example, a boutique could use AI to identify popular products and optimal promotion times, while a café might analyze foot traffic and weather patterns to predict busy periods. AI helps organize and interpret large amounts of data, enabling informed decisions about inventory, marketing, and more. This efficient use of analytics, empowered by AI, can lead to improved operations, marketing effectiveness, and overall business growth.

Conclusion: Harnessing the Power of Data for Business Growth

In Hackensack's dynamic environment, staying informed and agile is key to business success. Embracing analytics empowers your business with the knowledge to make smarter decisions, better understand your customers, and strategically navigate the market. Let data guide you to unlock new opportunities and achieve greater heights on Main Street.

CHAPTER 7: BUDGETING AND RESOURCE ALLOCATION FOR SMALL BUSINESSES ON MAIN STREET

Summary and Introduction: Strategic Financial Planning for Growth

In this chapter, we're diving into one of the trickiest yet most essential aspects of running a small business: figuring out where to allocate your money so it works the hardest for you. Whether you're serving the best coffee in town, connecting people with the latest tech, or dressing them in the latest styles, how you manage your budget can make or break your business.

First up, we'll talk about setting up a marketing budget. Think of it as walking a tightrope – balancing your ambitions with what your wallet can handle. Many small business owners don't have a formal marketing budget, which is a big mistake. You don't need anything fancy; it's just a simple plan to track your spending and its returns. I'll show you how to determine what portion of your revenue should go toward marketing – and it's probably more than you think. Plus, I'll help you ensure you're investing in the right areas.

Next, we'll explore how to make the most of what you've got, especially if you're working with a tight budget. I'm a big fan of clever, low-cost strategies that pack a punch without draining your bank account. Think social media magic, email marketing, and good old-fashioned community engagement. We'll also navigate the digital marketing jungle – from setting aside funds for online ads to managing website costs and SEO.

But here's the real kicker – as we say in the startup world, you must balance the quick wins with the slow burn. I'll help you understand the difference between marketing moves that give you an immediate boost and those that build your brand over time. And, of course, a very important part of managing your marketing budget is monitoring your marketing efforts, the related budget, and results, tweaking it, and continuing testing until you get it right. This way, you can ensure your marketing spend is always working as hard as you are.

Ready to turn your budget into your secret weapon? Let's make smart, strategic choices that align with your goals and financial reality. Let's get started!

1. Crafting a Realistic Marketing Budget

Did you pick up on the key word? Realistic. Creating a marketing budget is a balancing act between your business goals and financial realities. When it comes to a marketing budget for small business, you don't need a complex plan. All you need is a one-page spreadsheet to track your expenses, and the results are a good start.

- **Percentage of Revenue Approach:** Small business owners' first question about marketing is, "How much should I spend?" A good rule of thumb is to allocate 5-10% of your total revenue to marketing. I would bet this might be more than you expected, but it's necessary to drive growth.

- **Prioritizing Marketing Activities:** Focus on marketing activities that offer the highest return on investment. For example, a Hackensack restaurant might allocate more to local advertising and community events, while a retail store might invest in social media marketing and online ads. Prioritize spending based on what will give you the most significant impact. Of course, you need to decide what "impact" means to you. What are your goals? Revenue? Social followers? Visits to your store?

2. Maximizing Your Marketing Impact with Limited Resources

In my life, especially in Corporate America, I've had monster marketing budgets with massive spreadsheets to track everything. But, in small business efforts, effective marketing doesn't require a large budget.

- **Leveraging Low-Cost Digital Tools:** Use cost-effective digital marketing tools and platforms that offer high impact with low investment. Social media, email marketing, and basic SEO techniques are your friends here. These tools, covered in other parts of this book, allow you to reach a large audience without a price tag.

- **Community-Based Marketing:** This is where you can really stretch your marketing budget AND build community at the same time. Engage in grassroots efforts like participating in local events, networking, and word-of-mouth marketing. These strategies can be powerful and cost-effective in a community like Hackensack. Building relationships with local customers creates a loyal customer base.

3. Navigating the Costs of Digital Marketing

Digital marketing is effective but comes with its own set of costs. Understanding how to budget for these initiatives is crucial.

- **Allocating Funds for Online Advertising:** It's often that small business owners will eventually get around to wanting to advertise on digital channels, and this is an important part of where you can allocate part of your budget for online advertising, including social media ads and Google AdWords. Setting realistic goals and tracking ROI is important to ensure your spending is effective. If done correctly, online ads can drive significant traffic to your website or physical store. "Correctly" is the key word here, and I never suggest that small business owners start placing digital ads and boosting social media posts without knowing what they're doing. This is a good time to reach out for help. Find someone who is familiar with digital advertising to help you with your planning, efforts, and tracking. By the way, this doesn't mean you need to run out and hire a large, digital agency. There are plenty of smaller, more cost-effective options. This is where attending Chamber of Commerce meetings or events like my Small Business Meetups is important. Just remember, just running out and placing digital ads without knowing what you're doing won't work. Period. Seek out help with this one.

- **Website and SEO Costs:** As we've already discussed, a website is critical to your plan. But when planning your budget, you need to understand the costs of maintaining a website and implementing SEO strategies. These budget line items include web hosting fees (like rent for your digital store), design costs (like construction for that store), and potentially hiring SEO experts (making sure people can find your digital store). At the end of the day, a well-maintained website is crucial for attracting and retaining customers.

4. Balancing Between Short-Term and Long-Term Investments

In my thousands of conversations with small business owners, the biggest mistake I see people making is not understanding some marketing strategies yield immediate returns while others are long-term investments. Again, it's all about goals. What are you trying to accomplish? Your goals will determine how you budget for your activities.

- **Short-Term vs. Long-Term Marketing Strategies:** Distinguish between short-term tactics like seasonal promotions or flash sales and long-term strategies like brand awareness or SEO. Short-term strategies can boost sales quickly, while long-term strategies build a sustainable brand presence. Guess what? Overall, you need both, but it's a balancing act.

- **Allocating Budget for Long-Term Growth:** You must allocate a portion of your budget towards long-term goals to ensure sustained growth and market presence. Again, marketing is a dial you can turn up or down. It shouldn't be "on or off." Investing in long-term strategies will pay off over time through brand loyalty and consistent customer engagement – having long-term, repeat customers.

5. Tracking and Adjusting Your Marketing Budget

A marketing budget requires regular review and adjustments to stay effective.

- **Monitoring Marketing Expenses:** Implement systems to track and compare your marketing expenses against results. Even the most basic, rudimentary tracking helps you make informed decisions about where to adjust spending. Regular monitoring also ensures you're not wasting money on ineffective strategies. So, I'm all for boosting social media posts, but what are you trying to accomplish with that spend? Getting more followers? Achieving more sales? What? How can you determine if marketing expenses are worth it if you're not measuring results?

- **Flexible Budgeting for Changing Market Dynamics:** The second most common mistake is not constantly testing and adjusting your marketing efforts and the related costs. Track results and be prepared to adjust your budget in response to market changes, new opportunities, or shifts in customer behavior. Flexibility allows you to capitalize on the latest trends and avoid potential pitfalls. Now, be careful here. You also need to give things time to work. For me, I've always looked at this as a dial versus a switch. Try things, test, track results, and tweak. Give things time and give yourself a chance to make small changes to get results.

6. Budgeting Success Stories

- **'Bistro Bonanza':** A local restaurant allocated a significant portion of its budget to sponsor a popular local event, resulting in extensive media coverage and increased new customers. This strategic move boosted their visibility and customer base.

- **'Gadget Central':** A small tech store redirected its budget from traditional advertising to social media campaigns, leading to a stronger online presence and increased sales. This shift allowed them to reach a broader audience more effectively.

AI Topic: Using AI to Help with Your Budget

AI in budgeting transforms how small businesses allocate resources. For instance, if you run a boutique, AI can predict which product lines will likely demand more, helping you allocate funds more efficiently. AI can analyze sales data to suggest the best times for promotional campaigns, ensuring you get the most bang for your buck. AI-driven tools provide insights into customer spending patterns, allowing you to effectively tailor inventory and marketing efforts. Now, if you've read this AI paragraph and said to yourself, "That's way too complicated for me."

Conclusion: Your Blueprint for Financial Mastery in Marketing

Effective budgeting and resource allocation involves making strategic decisions aligned with your business goals and financial capabilities. A thoughtful approach to your marketing spend can pave the way for sustained growth and success in Hackensack, where every dollar counts. Embrace these strategies to make informed financial decisions that propel your business forward on Main Street.

MARKETING ON MAIN STREET

CHAPTER 8: STRATEGIC PARTNERSHIPS AND COLLABORATIONS

Building Synergistic Business Relationships

If you've looked into my work, you might know I'm working on another book, "Creating Winning Strategic Partnerships." That book dives into the details of forming strategic partnerships, from the initial vision to pitching, contracting, and implementation. It's geared towards medium and large businesses, so you might not need it now. However, it's important to note that every project I've worked on professionally has involved strategic partners. You can achieve your goals faster and with less risk with the right partner. As the Executive Director of the Main Street Business Alliance, I see this need in Special Improvement Districts, too.

Every connection can lead to new opportunities in a diverse business environment. Strategic partnerships and collaborations are powerful tools for your small business's growth and innovation. Whether running a restaurant, a mobile phone store, or a dress shop, forming alliances can significantly enhance your reach and impact. This chapter offers a roadmap to building successful partnerships and collaborations in Hackensack.

1. The Power of Strategic Partnerships

Partnerships and collaborations can enhance your business capabilities by offering complementary products or services, reaching new customer segments, and sharing marketing efforts. The bottom line? Partnering up can help your business grow quickly, cost-effectively, and with less risk.

Identifying Potential Partnerships: Look for partners whose values align with yours and whose offerings complement your own. For example, a café could partner with a local bookstore for a combined reading and dining experience. Femme, a women-only gym, might collaborate with restaurants and juice cafés that offer healthy meals and smoothies. You're not competing; you're targeting a similar audience together.

Benefits of Collaborative Efforts:

- **Diverse Market Reach:** Hackensack's community, for example, mixes young professionals, baby boomers, and diverse ethnic backgrounds.

Collaborating with another business to cross-promote can help you reach a wider audience. Imagine a dress shop partnering with a local nail salon for a bridal event, a vitamin store, and a health food café creating joint wellness programs. These partnerships open new market segments.

- **Community Building and Customer Loyalty:** Collaborations foster a sense of community. Businesses supporting each other create a supportive network that resonates with customers. People love seeing their favorite local businesses team up, strengthening their loyalty and encouraging a 'support local' mindset.

- **Shared Resources and Cost Efficiency:** Small businesses often face budget constraints. By pooling resources, companies can share costs for marketing campaigns, events, or joint purchases. For example, a group of restaurants could band together to buy in bulk, reducing costs. Shared resources also mean shared risks, making new ventures more accessible and less daunting.

- **Innovation through Combined Expertise:** Every business brings unique strengths. A jeweler might excel in visual merchandising, while a mobile phone store might be great at digital marketing. Companies can leverage each other's strengths by collaborating, leading to innovative solutions.

- **Enhanced Online Presence and Social Media Engagement:** Today's active online presence is crucial. Collaborative efforts, like joint social media campaigns or shared online content, can significantly increase reach and engagement. For instance, a collaborative Instagram giveaway between a clothing store and a barber shop can drive followers and engagement for both parties.

Remember, collaboration is about building bridges. In a community as diverse and dynamic as Hackensack, one's success can fuel the success of all. Let's embrace the power of working together and watch our businesses and community flourish.

2. Crafting Mutually Beneficial Partnerships

The best partnerships are those in which all parties gain value. These win-win relationships may not always be perfectly balanced, but they work if everyone gets what they want.

Defining Partnership Goals: Clearly define each party's hopes to achieve, whether increased sales, market exposure, or shared customer bases. This is a critical first step.

Structuring the Partnership: Look into different ways to structure collaborations, such as joint events, cross-promotions, or shared loyalty programs.

3. Effective Communication and Relationship Management

Maintaining a healthy partnership requires open communication and aligned goals.

Regular Check-ins and Updates: Establish a routine for regular meetings and updates to ensure all parties are on the same page and satisfied with the partnership's progress.

Resolving Conflicts: Done properly, strategic partnerships are a wonderful way to achieve the goals you've set out for yourself. However, every once in a while, a partnership isn't going to go as planned. Hey, it happens. When it does, get together with your strategic partner and offer strategies for constructively resolving disagreements or misalignments. The worst thing you can do is avoid the issue. See a problem? Jump on it. Likely, it's just a communication issue, and you'll be able to solve the problem and maintain the relationship. If not, and something that is a deal-breaker comes up, rip the band-aid off and sever the relationship by parting ways amicably. Don't write off strategic partnerships entirely. You tried one and learned from it. The next one will be better.

4. Local Collaborations for Community Engagement

Community-centric collaborations can be particularly effective in places like Hackensack and other cities with many small businesses in one area, such as Main Street.

Community-Centric Collaborations at Local Events: Explore ideas for collaborations that resonate with the community, such as participating in local festivals. Each October in Hackensack, the Main Street Business Alliance has an outdoor event called Hackensacktoberfest. We encourage local businesses to participate and love it when small businesses join forces to offer promotions. or community service projects.

5. Evaluating and Measuring the Success of Partnerships

Not all partnerships will succeed; measuring and evaluating their effectiveness is essential. However, they are guaranteed to fail if you never try them. The MSBA can help you put together collaborations on Main Street. And, if you're reading this in some other city in the US, I'm always happy to consult with you to brainstorm ideas about how you can grow your business with the help of a strategic partner.

Setting Metrics for Success: Determine how you will measure the partnership's success, whether through increased sales, customer feedback, or other metrics. It might even be website traffic or email signups. Please keep it simple, though. If you make the metrics too complicated, you're destined not to track them at all.

Review and Adjust: A strategic partnership is a plan to jointly work on something together, be it a promotion or some other project. But partnerships, like anything else, are rarely perfect. So, be prepared to review the partnership regularly and make adjustments as needed to ensure it continues to be mutually beneficial. It's okay to zig and zag as you work together. Frankly, that's the fun part.

6. Hackensack Success Stories: Real-Life Collaborative Wins

Community Engagement and New Cuisine: At the Main Street Business Alliance, we're always working on ways to get residents (new and legacy ones) to try the new restaurants on Main Street. So, we partnered with the award-winning Johnson Public Library to launch "Games on Main," a free, monthly game night where we invite everyone in the community to come out to a different restaurant to play board games and enjoy some light food. It's a wonderful program that benefits the restaurant, the Library, the Alliance, AND the community. Boosting visibility for everyone involved is a win that otherwise wouldn't have been achieved.

Pet Care-Photography Fusion: Roberto and Toni from SUNMED have pet-centric products to calm anxious dogs. They partnered with a photographer looking to expand her customer base by hosting an event promoting the CBD pet product AND offering free pet photos. It was a wonderful collaboration showcasing a pet-related product and a photography service aimed at pet lovers, which attracted a diverse crowd and social media attention.

Using AI to Find and Nurture the Right Strategic Partnership

AI can significantly aid in identifying and managing strategic partnerships. Imagine you own a fitness studio; AI can analyze local business synergies and suggest potential partners, like a health food café. It can even help monitor the success of these collaborations by tracking joint marketing campaign performances and customer cross-engagement. AI-driven analysis can ensure that partnerships are fruitful and align well with your business goals and values. The end of the book features a resource section where you can find various AI tools to use for almost any scenario.

Conclusion: Cultivating Collaborative Growth

In Hackensack or any other city, you'll find vibrant and cooperative environments where strategic partnerships and collaborations can enhance your business's potential. They go beyond shared costs or resources; they build relationships that foster growth, innovation, and community engagement. Embrace the power of collaboration and watch as it transforms your business and contributes to the vibrant tapestry of your business community.

CHAPTER 9: IMPLEMENTING FUTURE MARKETING TRENDS FOR SMALL BUSINESS

Summary and Introduction: Navigating the Ever-Changing Landscape of Marketing

Welcome to a chapter filled with practical insights! As we delve into this content, envision yourself navigating the ever-changing marketing landscape in a bustling city like Hackensack – or, better yet, your community. This chapter isn't just about abstract ideas; it's about translating these concepts into actionable steps for your business. Whether you're a local burger place or a trendy CBD retailer, the strategies we'll explore, inspired by successful companies like Marty's Burgers and SUNMED, are designed to help you thrive.

In today's diverse business environment, staying on top of emerging marketing trends is a game-changer. The first step is wanting to start; the second is knowing where to begin. Ignoring new technology and sticking to old-school strategies might work for a while, but eventually, you'll fall behind. (Apologies for the bluntness – I'm from Jersey!) If you're not tech-savvy, don't worry; we're here to guide you. Additionally, we'll guide you on finding and applying for grants and funding opportunities, making investing in these new marketing strategies easier.

1. Incorporating Augmented Reality (AR) in Marketing

Augmented Reality (AR) uniquely engages customers by blending the digital and physical worlds. Think it's not for you? Read on.

Identifying Opportunities: Imagine the possibilities for your small business. Picture a local fashion boutique using AR for virtual try-ons. Customers could see how clothes look on them without trying them on physically. AR isn't just for big companies – it's a tool that can also level the playing field for small businesses. From seeing what a hat looks like on your head to visualizing a new chair in your living room, AR is a practical and accessible tool that enhances customer experience. Even local signage companies can benefit by showing potential clients what their new storefront sign would look like. This customization turns potential customers into real ones, opening up a world of new opportunities for your business.

Developing the AR Experience: You have two practical options. First, collaborate with an AR developer to create something for your website or app. Second, use DIY tools like Zapworks Designer, a no-code AR software that makes creating immersive web-based AR experiences straightforward. Ensure whatever you build is user-friendly and adds value to the customer experience. Have you used social media filters on Instagram or Snapchat? Those are AR filters, so don't be intimidated – start experimenting. With these practical steps, you can take control of your marketing strategy and stay ahead of the game.

2. Implementing Eco-Friendly Marketing Initiatives

If you're skeptical about sustainability, consider the growing number of customers who value eco-friendliness. Implementing eco-friendly marketing can enhance your brand's appeal and demonstrate social responsibility. However, it's important to know the potential challenges of implementing these initiatives, such as bag-free shopping. Understanding these challenges can help you prepare and overcome them.

Developing a Green Branding Strategy:

Audit Current Practices: Making your business more sustainable is easier than you think. Assess your business practices for sustainability. This could mean sourcing eco-friendly materials or improving energy efficiency. Authenticity is key; you need to walk the talk. These steps benefit the environment, enhance your brand's appeal, and demonstrate social responsibility.

Communicate Your Green Efforts: Use your website, social media, and in-store signage to inform customers about your eco-friendly practices. Highlight efforts like using locally sourced, organic ingredients or local recycling programs. Effectively communicating your green efforts will help you build customer trust and loyalty.

Hosting Sustainable Events:

Plan Eco-friendly Events: For instance, a café could host a workshop on sustainable brewing practices and, at the same time, showcase the eco-friendly cups they use or the fact they don't even use paper cups for "dine in" customers.

Promote Your Event: Use social media, community boards, and partnerships with eco-conscious local businesses. Collaborating with other companies can enhance the event's reach and impact. And, if you partner with the right organization, you'll even legitimize your efforts in the eyes of existing and potential customers.

3. Personalized Marketing Using Data Analytics

Personalized marketing can significantly improve customer engagement and loyalty. Imagine the impact of customized emails tailored to customer preferences. They are far more effective than generic messages, showing your customers you understand and value their needs. This can increase customer loyalty and repeat business, boosting your bottom line. By using AI, you can change boring, generic email blasts to fine-tuned, customized communication vehicles. I can tell you from personal experience that lately, the customized email pitches I receive have been far more interesting than email promotions that invade my inbox.

Collecting and Utilizing Customer Data:

Data Collection Methods: Use tools like Google Analytics and social media insights. Simple methods like feedback forms and online surveys with incentives can also gather valuable information. Purchase history is key for personalizing offers, which impress customers and show them you value their patronage.

Implement Personalization: Use data to tailor marketing efforts. For example, create targeted email campaigns based on customer preferences and purchase history. If a regular customer hasn't visited in a while, a personalized message can re-engage them. An email that starts with "Hey John! We haven't seen you in a while, so we're sending you this discount code to get you to try our new line of car care products" is far more effective than a generic offer of "10% off Car Care Products." Developing a customized marketing strategy helps you engage your customers more effectively.

Creating Personalized Customer Experiences:

Customer Segmentation: Personalized marketing efforts don't always mean one-on-one messaging. Segmenting your customers based on preferences, behaviors, and purchase history is also effective. Tailor your campaigns to speak directly to these segments rather than a broad audience. For instance, a jewelry store could send exclusive offers to high-spending customers. An office supply company could send exclusive offers on ink and paper to customers who have recently bought a printer.

4. Effective Use of Influencer Marketing

Influencer marketing, covered in detail in the Social Media chapter, can connect you with new audiences.

Influencers have a strong social media presence and can influence consumer views and purchasing decisions.

Identifying and Collaborating with Influencers:

Research Potential Influencers: Look for local influencers whose followers match your target demographic. Tools like BuzzSumo or HypeAuditor can help.

Establishing Collaborations: Contact influencers with clear proposals for collaborations, such as sponsored posts or joint events. Any influencer who is open to 'collab' requests already says they'd consider working with you, so don't hesitate to reach out.

Measuring the Impact:

Set Clear Goals: Define what success looks like, whether it's increased brand awareness, more followers, or higher sales.

Track and Analyze: Use analytics tools to monitor metrics like engagement rates, website traffic from influencer links, and sales. This will help you measure the success of your marketing strategies and make necessary adjustments to improve your results.

5. Adapting to Market Changes with Agile Marketing

Agile marketing allows you to quickly adapt to changing market trends and consumer behaviors. It requires flexibility and a willingness to experiment.

Staying Informed on Market Trends:

Regular Research: Follow marketing trends through online resources, trade publications, and local business networks. Tools like Google Trends can provide insights. Reading daily newsletters, of which there are many, like "The Brew" can also keep you informed. Check out my website johntpeters.com for tips on how to stay updated on emerging marketing trends, ensuring you always stay ahead of the curve. Specifically, there's a post titled "What I read" I think you'll find of interest.

Attending Workshops, Seminars, and Meetups: Participate in local workshops or online webinars focused on marketing trends. I host a small business meetup with a different theme each month. Topics might include how to get the most out of working with Instagram influencers or the best way to find grants for your business. The point is if you sit in your business and do the same thing, day in and day out, you will achieve the same results. Get out and learn new things. Sure, it takes time out of your day, but you'll get something out of it, even if it's just a few ideas of new things to try.

Walk Before You Run - Implementing Agile Marketing Strategies:

Quick Response, Test, and Learn: Develop a flexible marketing strategy to capitalize on new trends quickly. Set aside a budget for experimental marketing tactics. I usually put aside 10% of my marketing budget for "testing." Testing new approaches on a small scale, assessing their effectiveness, and then deciding what to integrate into your broader strategy is always a great way to limit spending on tactics that don't pan out. For example, if I don't see the results I was hoping for after testing a marketing tactic, I pivot and tweak the effort. If, after another test, I still don't see the results I wanted, I try something else entirely. Utilizing a flexible marketing strategy helps you adapt to changing market trends and consumer behaviors. If you come away with anything from this book, it should be the concept of testing and tweaking to get things right and, if they ultimately don't, cut the effort in time to try another one.

How AI Might Help with Marketing

AI can be a powerful ally in predicting and adapting to future trends. For example, AI can analyze global and local digital trends, helping you stay ahead of the curve. It can identify upcoming social media platforms and predict new consumer behavior patterns, giving you the foresight to adapt your strategies proactively. AI equips you with the tools to stay relevant and competitive.

Conclusion: Charting Your Marketing Future

As markets in cities like Hackensack evolve, so do the opportunities to connect with and engage your customers. By embracing these future marketing trends and learning to implement them effectively, your business can stay ahead in a competitive landscape. Remember, the future of marketing isn't just about following trends; it's about creatively adapting them to fit your unique business and audience. Let's start and chart a vibrant, dynamic course for your marketing future!

CHAPTER 10: GRANTS AND FUNDING OPPORTUNITIES FOR HACKENSACK BUSINESSES

Summary: Unlocking Financial Growth through Grants

In this chapter, we dive into a crucial topic for small businesses on Main Street – grants and funding. Whether you run a local health food store, a tech shop, or a fashion boutique, understanding grants can be your ticket to financial growth and stability.

We'll explore the landscape of business grants and opportunities with specific criteria and requirements. I'll guide you through the different types of grants available – from federal to local, and special grants for minority or woman-owned businesses. Knowing where to look and how to find the right grants is key.

Next, we'll tackle the grant application process. This might seem daunting, but don't worry – I'll provide a step-by-step guide. From gathering essential documents to understanding each grant's requirements, we'll walk through crafting a compelling proposal. This includes writing an executive summary, detailing your business and project plans, and presenting a concise budget.

Local and state grants often focus on community impact and can be less competitive than federal grants. We'll delve into resources like the Main Street Business Alliance and Bergen County's offerings, highlighting how to emphasize your business's contribution to Hackensack's vibrant community.

Getting the grant is just the beginning. Managing these funds effectively is crucial. I'll show you how to set up a tracking system to ensure every dollar is accounted for and used as intended. Staying true to your proposal and complying with the grant's conditions is essential.

Finally, we'll talk about the importance of reporting and compliance. Most grants require you to report on how you've used the funds. It's about maintaining transparency and building a track record of responsible and effective grant usage.

As we conclude this chapter, remember that navigating the world of grants is more than securing funding. It's about learning, growing, and opening new doors for your business in Hackensack. Let's get started and unlock these opportunities for your business to thrive on Main Street!

1. Understanding the Landscape of Business Grants

Grants are free money offered to businesses, typically by government entities, corporations, or foundations, but they come with specific criteria and obligations.

Identify Grant Types: Various grants include federal, state, local, and private grants. Special grants are available for minority-owned, woman-owned, and small businesses.

Researching Grants: Utilize online databases such as Grants.gov, local government websites, or business associations like the Main Street Business Alliance for grant opportunities. Networking with other local business owners can also provide leads.

2. The Grant Application Process: A Step-by-Step Guide

Securing a grant requires careful preparation and a strategic approach to the application process.

Preparing for the Application:

Document Gathering: Organize essential documents like your business plan, financial statements, tax returns, and proof of business registration.

Understanding the Grant Requirements: Read the grant application thoroughly to understand what it entails. Note specific requirements such as business size, industry type, and intended use of funds.

Writing a Grant Proposal:

Executive Summary: Begin with a compelling executive summary that briefly outlines your business and why it deserves the grant.

Business Description: Provide a detailed description of your business, including its history, mission, target market, and products/services.

Project Description: Clearly outline the project or purpose for which you need the grant. Explain how it aligns with the grant's objectives.

Budget Plan: Include a detailed budget that shows how the grant funds will be used. Be transparent and realistic about your financial needs and projections.

3. Finding Local and State Grant Opportunities

Local and state grants often focus on community impact, making them an excellent fit for small businesses.

Local and State Resources:

Main Street Business Alliance: Explore programs and grants available through the Main Street Business Alliance.

Bergen County Grants: Check Bergen County's website for business grants to support local economic growth.

Crafting a Community Impact Statement:

Highlight Community Contributions: Emphasize how your business supports the local community, creates jobs, and contributes to the economy.

Focus on Local Benefits: Tailor your proposal to reflect how the grant will enhance your business's ability to serve Hackensack and its residents.

4. Managing and Tracking Grant Funds

Effective management and tracking of grant funds ensure compliance and success.

Set Up a Tracking System: Use accounting software or a spreadsheet to monitor grant fund usage. Categorize expenses according to the grant's budget plan.

Stay True to Your Proposal: Ensure you spend the funds outlined in your grant proposal. Avoid deviating from your stated plan without proper approval.

Complying with Conditions: Understand and adhere to all conditions set by the grant provider, including spending limits, timelines, and reporting requirements.

5. Reporting and Compliance

Most grants require periodic reporting to track progress and fund usage.

Prepare Regular Reports:

Document Your Progress: Keep detailed records of how grant funds are being used and the progress of your project.

Meet Reporting Deadlines: Submit all required reports on time. Use these reports to highlight your achievements and any challenges faced.

Maintain Transparency:

Be Honest and Accurate: Ensure all information provided in reports is accurate and truthful. Transparency builds trust and can increase your chances of securing future grants.

Build a Track Record: A history of successful grant management and compliance can enhance your reputation and make it easier to obtain future funding.

AI Topic: Using AI to Find Grants

AI can be a powerful ally for business owners, even when trying to find grants to apply for. AI-driven tools can scour through vast databases of available grants, filtering opportunities that align with a business's specific needs and qualifications. This will save you some time, but more importantly, it will help you find the best grants. AI can also assist in the application process by analyzing previous successful applications to suggest effective wording and key points. Additionally, AI can keep track of deadlines and requirements for each grant, ensuring applications are complete and submitted on time. This tailored approach simplifies the often complex and time-consuming process of grant applications, allowing small business owners to focus more on their business operations while maximizing their chances of securing funding.

Conclusion: Harnessing Grants for Business Advancement in Hackensack

Navigating the world of grants and funding is a journey of learning and opportunity. The first step is understanding the types of grants available to you and your business. Then, you must master the application process; unfortunately, this takes practice. The process is sometimes arduous, but you'll get the hang of it. Then, it would be best to ensure you're effectively managing and reporting progress on the grant funds you received. This way, your Hackensack business can leverage these resources for significant growth and development. Embrace this journey as an integral part of your business strategy, and let it open new doors to success and sustainability on Main Street.

CHAPTER 11:
MASTERING OFFLINE MARKETING IN HACKENSACK

Summary and Introduction: The Power of Traditional Marketing

Welcome to Chapter 12! While the digital world continues to grow and evolve, the enduring charm and effectiveness of offline marketing remain vital. Whether crafting the best pancakes in town, repairing the latest gadgets, or outfitting Hackensack most finely, mastering traditional marketing techniques can elevate your local presence. This chapter is your comprehensive guide to navigating and leveraging these timeless strategies, especially if you're new to offline marketing.

Effective Use of Signage and Local Advertising

Your journey begins with the cornerstone of offline marketing: impactful signage and local advertising. Signage is more than a mere label; it's a silent ambassador for your brand. I'll guide you through designing signage that captures the essence of your business while respecting the architectural harmony of Hackensack. The goal is to be bold and visible yet in tune with the community's aesthetic.

I spend much time working with the Main Street Business Alliance (MSBA) in Hackensack, helping business owners like you strike the perfect balance between standing out and fitting in. And guess what? Financial assistance is available for this, too!

Designing Impactful Signage:

- **Choose Strategic Locations:** Place your signs where they'll be most visible to both foot and vehicle traffic. Consider factors like height, lighting, and potential obstructions.

- **Design Tips:** Use clear, readable fonts and appealing colors that reflect your brand's personality. For example, a quirky design might suit a café, while a sleek look would be ideal for a tech store.

- **Include Essential Information:** Ensure your sign includes your business name, logo, and a concise tagline explaining what your business offers. Additionally, remember to follow local ordinances regarding the placement of building numbers and business hours.

Embracing Elegance and Respect in Signage:

In the heart of Hackensack, NJ, Main Street is a vibrant mix of historic charm and modern flair. Understanding the "art of signage" is crucial for new business owners. It's not just about catching the eye but respecting the community's vision and adhering to local ordinances.

The MSBA plays a pivotal role in guiding this vision. We're not just about enforcement; we offer incentives. Through façade and signage improvement grants, the MSBA aims to revitalize the business district, enhance shopping experiences, and foster a cohesive streetscape. You can explore these resources, including detailed guidelines and grant applications, at www.downtownhackensack.org.

Remember that Hackensack is a tapestry of history, diversity, and modernity when designing your signage. Your sign should blend into this fabric while standing out for its class and clarity. Avoid common pitfalls like flashing lights or cluttered displays, which don't conform to local regulations and can detract from the overall appeal.

Your sign respectfully nods to both the past and the future. Adhere to local ordinances, seek guidance from the

MSBA, and create a sign as elegant and welcoming as Hackensack.

Local Advertising Tactics:

- **Newspaper and Radio:** Contact local newspapers and radio stations for advertising opportunities. Craft ads that resonate with the Hackensack community and emphasize your unique selling points.

- **Community Boards and Flyers:** Utilize community bulletin boards in libraries, community centers, and grocery stores. Distribute flyers in high foot traffic areas, ensuring you obtain permission from store owners for in-window displays.

Hosting and Participating in Local Events

Events are a fantastic way to engage directly with the community and promote your business.

Joining Community Events:

- **Research Local Events:** Look for street fairs, festivals, and markets where you can set up a booth or offer your products/services. Hackensacktoberfest is an ideal example, among many others listed on www.DowntownHackensack.org.

- **Participation Strategy:** Plan how to engage attendees with product demonstrations, free samples, or promotional giveaways.

Organizing Your Events:

- **Event Planning:** Host events that align with your business. For instance, a bookstore might organize a local author's book signing, or a café might host live music nights.
- **Promotion:** Advertise your event through local media, social media, in-store signage, and word-of-mouth.

Leveraging Local Media and Word-of-Mouth

Local media and word-of-mouth are powerful tools for building your business's reputation in Hackensack.

Engaging with Local Media:

- **Press Releases:** Send press releases to local newspapers and magazines to announce significant events, new products, or business milestones.
- **Community Features:** Participate in community stories or segments highlighting local businesses.

Encouraging Word-of-Mouth:

- **Deliver Exceptional Service:** Provide experiences that make customers want to discuss your business.
- **Incentivize Referrals:** Offer incentives for customers who refer friends and family, such as discounts or loyalty points.

Building Customer Loyalty Through Offline Channels

Establishing a loyal customer base is essential for long-term success.

Loyalty Programs:
- **Implement a Loyalty System:** Create a program that rewards repeat business, like a punch card system for a café or a points program for a retail store.
- **Promote Your Program:** Ensure customers know your loyalty program. Train your staff to explain it to customers and promote it at the point of sale.

Personalized Customer Service:
- **Know Your Customers:** Make an effort to remember regular customers' names and preferences. Personal touches can turn a casual

customer into a loyal one. For example, owner LeVar Thomas greets his regulars by name at Iconic Coffee in Hackensack and remembers their usual orders.

Using AI to Enhance Your Offline Strategy

AI can be crucial in enhancing offline marketing strategies for small businesses. AI can analyze customer data and local market trends to suggest the most effective offline marketing tactics, such as community events, local sponsorships, or direct mail campaigns. For instance, a local bookstore could use AI to determine the ideal neighborhoods for a direct mail campaign based on reading preferences and purchasing habits. Additionally, AI can measure the impact of offline marketing efforts by correlating them with changes in in-store traffic and sales, providing valuable feedback for future campaigns. This integration allows small businesses to make data-driven decisions, ensuring their efforts are effective and efficiently targeted.

Conclusion: Embracing Offline Marketing for Business Growth

In the diverse and dynamic environment of Hackensack, offline marketing remains a vital tool for connecting with the community, building brand awareness, and fostering customer loyalty. By implementing these detailed strategies, you can create a strong offline presence that complements your digital marketing efforts, paving the way for a thriving business on Main Street. Let's step out from behind the screens and make your mark in the streets of Hackensack – where real, lasting business relationships are forged.

CHAPTER 12: ENGAGING YOUR COMMUNITY THROUGH EVENTS AND SPONSORSHIPS

Summary and Introduction: Strengthening Your Local Ties in Hackensack

Welcome to Chapter 13! In Hackensack, every small business – from your cozy café to your bustling mobile phone store – is a vital part of the local community. Engaging with the community goes beyond marketing; it's about building real, heartfelt connections. This chapter is packed with insights on planning, hosting, and making the most of community events and sponsorships, especially if you're new.

Picture your café alive with a coffee-tasting event or your chic boutique turning into a runway for a local fashion show. This chapter will guide you through creating such memorable community events. It's about choosing events that showcase what you do best and resonate with Hackensack's spirit. I'll walk you through the logistics, budgeting, and promotion, ensuring your events create lasting impressions.

We'll also dive into local sponsorships, where supporting community activities intersects with boosting your business's visibility. You'll learn to find sponsorship opportunities that align with your values and appeal to your clientele, making your brand an active part of the community.

Workshops and classes are other powerful tools. They're not just educational sessions; they position your business as a source of knowledge and expertise. Whether it's a tech workshop or a craft class, I'll show you how to select topics, plan sessions, and promote them to attract eager participants.

Participation in community events is also crucial. This chapter will teach you how to choose the right events, design a compelling booth, and engage attendees in ways that leave a lasting impression.

Lastly, we'll discuss measuring success and learning from each event. This involves gathering feedback, evaluating outcomes, and fine-tuning your strategy. Every event is an opportunity to grow closer to the community and enhance your business.

Engaging your community through events and sponsorships is an art. It's about more than just business growth; it's about embedding your business into the very soul of Hackensack, building relationships that transcend transactions. This chapter guides you to become a true pillar of the Hackensack community.

1. Planning and Hosting Memorable Community Events

Events are a dynamic way to engage directly with your customers and create unforgettable experiences.

Identifying the Type of Event:

- **Consider Your Business Type:** Think about what makes your business unique. A café might host a coffee-tasting or latte art workshop, while a clothing store could organize a local fashion show.
- **Align with Community Interests:** Choose events that resonate with the Hackensack community. Seasonal festivals, cultural celebrations, or charity fundraisers can be great options.

Organizing the Event:

- **Logistics:** Choose a date and time that doesn't clash with other community events. Plan the layout, necessary equipment, and staffing.
- **Budgeting:** Create a budget including decorations, refreshments, and promotional materials.

- **Promotion:** Promote your event using local media, social media, in-store signage, and word-of-mouth. Collaborate with other businesses for cross-promotion.

2. Collaborating on Local Sponsorships

Sponsorships allow you to support community activities while increasing your business's visibility.

Finding Sponsorship Opportunities:

- **Local Research:** Look for local events, teams, or organizations that need sponsors. These could be anything from a local sports team to a community theater production.
- **Evaluating Fit:** Ensure the sponsorship opportunity aligns with your business values and appeals to your customer base.

Maximizing Sponsorship Impact:

- **Visibility:** Negotiate for visible branding opportunities during the event. This could include banners, program mentions, or branded merchandise.
- **Engagement:** Set up a booth to distribute informational materials about your business and give away samples to engage with attendees actively.

3. Running Successful Workshops and Classes

Workshops and classes provide value to attendees and position your business as a knowledgeable leader in your field.

Developing Your Workshop:

- **Topic Selection:** Choose topics that showcase your expertise and interest your customer base. For example, a tech store could offer classes on the latest software or gadgets.

- **Planning the Session:** Prepare an outline of what you will cover, including any hands-on activities or demonstrations. Ensure you have all the necessary materials and equipment.

Promoting Your Workshop:

- **In-store and Online Promotion:** Advertise your workshop using in-store displays and online platforms, including your website and social media.

- **Registration:** Set up a simple registration process in-store or through an online platform like Eventbrite.

4. Leveraging Event Participation for Marketing

Participating in community events can be an excellent marketing opportunity.

Choosing Events to Participate In:
- **Research Community Calendars:** Look for events where your target audience will likely be present. Food festivals, local markets, or charity events are often good choices.
- **Booth Design and Setup:** Create an inviting booth space that reflects your brand. Include clear signage, product displays, and interactive elements.

Post-Event Engagement:
- **Follow-up:** Collect contact information from attendees for follow-up marketing. This could include sending a thank-you email, a special discount offer, or a newsletter signup.

5. Measuring Success and Learning from Each Event

After each event or sponsorship, assess its impact on your business.

Feedback and Evaluation:

- **Gather Feedback:** Ask attendees for their feedback through informal conversations or a short survey. For every event I hold, I have a sign that says, "Did you enjoy this event?" with a QR code linking to a survey.

- **Review Objectives:** Compare the event's outcomes to your initial goals. Did you increase brand awareness, gain new customers, or enhance community relationships?

Adjusting Future Strategies:

- **Learn and Adapt:** Use the insights gained to improve future events. Identify what worked well and what could be enhanced.

Using AI to Help with Events:

AI can be a great help if you're unsure where to start. It can analyze local demographics, interests, and attendance history to suggest event themes likely to attract a large audience. For instance, AI could help a café owner determine if a local art showcase or a live music evening would draw more patrons based on community interests. Furthermore, AI can optimize event marketing, identifying the best channels and times to promote events. AI can evaluate success post-event by analyzing attendance data and social media engagement, providing insights for future event planning. This data-driven approach ensures events are well-attended and resonate with the community.

Conclusion: Becoming a Pillar of the Hackensack Community

Engaging with your community through events and sponsorships is more than just business promotion; it's about building genuine connections and becoming an integral part of the Hackensack community. By following these detailed steps, your business will grow in visibility and the hearts of community members. Embrace these opportunities to make your mark on Main Street and beyond.

CHAPTER 13: CUSTOMER SERVICE EXCELLENCE ON MAIN STREET

Summary and Introduction: Crafting Exceptional Customer Experiences

Let's get straight to the point: customer service is everything. You can follow every other tip in this book, but if you miss the mark on customer service, you're wasting your time. In a vibrant city like Hackensack, every interaction is an opportunity. Whether serving the perfect cup of coffee, fixing the latest gadgets, or showcasing the season's hottest fashion, exceptional customer service is crucial for building a loyal customer base and boosting your brand's reputation. This chapter is my guide to mastering customer service, especially for those just starting to navigate the world of customer relations.

First, let's discuss why customer service is your business's lifeline. It's your first and last impression, the core of customer loyalty, and your go-to strategy for handling any concerns. I'll explain how I developed a customer-first mindset and learned to understand the unique needs of our Hackensack community. Is it quick service, a personal touch, or expert product knowledge they're looking for? Let's discover it together.

Next, we'll dive into training our teams – our business champions. Their interactions can leave a lasting impact on our customers. I'll show you how I conduct regular training sessions focusing on communication skills and product knowledge and create a positive work environment where my staff feels valued and motivated.

Creating a customer-friendly atmosphere is not just about looks but the vibe. Whether it's the cozy seating in my café or the interactive tech area in your store, the environment you create plays a huge role in customer experience. I'll share how simple gestures like a warm greeting or offering help can make a huge difference.

Feedback is a gift, and I'll tell you how to set up multiple channels for it. From comment cards to social media, always actively seek out what customers think and use their feedback as a springboard for growth.

Handling complaints is an art, and I'll guide you through it. How I manage complaints has turned some of my most dissatisfied customers into my most loyal ones. I'll go through how I developed a complaint resolution process and empowered my staff to resolve issues swiftly and empathetically.

Going above and beyond – that's where the magic happens. It's about personalizing customer experiences and surprising them with delightful gestures. I'll share how these tactics can turn satisfied customers into passionate advocates for your brand.

Lastly, I'll explore how great customer service is an incredible marketing tool. I always encourage word-of-mouth, showcase my commitment to service on social media, and let my customers' testimonials speak for themselves. It would be best if you did the same.

As I wrap up this chapter and this book, I want to emphasize that in Hackensack, setting the bar high in customer service is the key to business success. It's more than transactions; it's about building relationships, creating memorable experiences, and becoming an integral part of our vibrant community. So, let's take this journey together and make our customer service a standout part of our customers' Hackensack experience.

1. Understanding the Importance of Customer Service

Customer service is the direct link between your business and your customers. It's crucial for first impressions, building loyalty, and handling concerns.

Develop a Customer-First Philosophy:

- Adopt a mindset where customer needs and satisfaction are a priority. Train your staff to approach every interaction with this philosophy.

Identify Your Customers' Needs:

- Spend time understanding what your Hackensack customers value. Is it quick service, personal attention, product knowledge, or something else?

2. Training Your Team for Service Excellence

Your staff are the ambassadors of your business. Their interactions with customers can leave a lasting impression.

Conduct Regular Training Sessions:

- Organize workshops focusing on communication skills, product knowledge, and handling difficult situations. Role-playing scenarios can be particularly effective.

Foster a Positive Work Environment:

• Happy employees often lead to happy customers. Create an environment where your staff feels valued and motivated.

3. Creating a Customer-Friendly Atmosphere

Your business's physical and emotional environment significantly influences customer experience.

Designing Your Space:

• Ensure your business is welcoming and comfortable. This includes clean, well-organized spaces and clear signage. A café might have cozy seating areas, while a tech store could have a tech demo area.

Building a Welcoming Culture:

• Encourage staff to greet customers warmly and be ready to assist. Small gestures like acknowledging customers as they enter can make a big difference.

4. Implementing Effective Feedback Mechanisms

Feedback is a gift. It helps you understand customer preferences and address issues.

Setting Up Feedback Channels:
- Provide multiple ways for customers to give feedback, such as comment cards, a section on your website, or through social media.

Actively Seeking Feedback:
- Don't wait for customers to provide feedback. Train your staff to ask customers about their experiences and suggest improvements.

5. Handling Complaints and Service Recovery

How you handle complaints can significantly impact customer perceptions and loyalty.

Develop a Complaint Resolution Process:
- Create clear guidelines for handling complaints. This should include listening attentively, empathizing with the customer, and offering solutions.

Empower Your Employees:

- Give your staff the authority to handle minor complaints on the spot. This could be processing a return, offering a discount, or providing a complimentary service.

6. Going Above and Beyond: Exceeding Expectations

Exceeding customer expectations can turn a satisfied customer into a loyal advocate.

Personalize the Customer Experience:

- Remember repeat customers and tailor services to their preferences. For instance, a restaurant might remember a regular's favorite dish.

Surprise and Delight Tactics:

- Occasionally offer something unexpected, like a free upgrade, a sample, or a small gift on special occasions.

7. Leveraging Customer Service for Marketing

Good customer service can be a powerful marketing tool.

Encourage Word-of-Mouth:

- Satisfied customers are your best advertising because they will most likely recommend your business to others.

Your goal? Encourage the spread of good news and referrals by providing excellent service worth discussing.

Showcase Your Commitment:

- Share stories of your excellent service on social media or in your marketing materials. Customer testimonials can be particularly effective.

Using AI to Transform Customer Service:

This chapter on customer service excellence, especially for small businesses, discusses how AI can be transformative. AI-enabled virtual assistants and chatbots can provide around-the-clock customer support, answering common questions and resolving simple issues. This enhances customer satisfaction and frees up human employees for more complicated tasks.

For example, a small retail store could use AI to handle frequently asked questions about store hours, product availability, or return policies. AI can also analyze customer feedback to identify common issues or trends, allowing businesses to address concerns and improve their service proactively. This AI toolset provides a proactive, data-driven approach to excellent customer service, streamlines operations, and significantly enhances the overall customer experience.

Conclusion: Setting the Standard in Customer Service

In Hackensack, where every customer counts, outstanding service can be the key to business success. By implementing the listed strategies, your business can create long-lasting customer relationships. Once you gain their trust, you'll earn their loyalty; they'll be your biggest advocates for your brand. Remember, in small businesses, exemplary customer service is not just a practice – it's a powerful tool for building your reputation and growing your presence in the community.

CHAPTER 14:
SOCIAL MEDIA MARKETING IN HACKENSACK'S BUSINESS LANDSCAPE

Summary and Introduction: Embracing the Social Media Revolution

Hello entrepreneurs! It's time to dive into the vibrant world of social media marketing. Social media is a game-changer whether you're dishing up the town's best eats, leading a cutting-edge tech shop, or running a chic boutique. But where do you start in this vast digital landscape? Right here! I'm about to guide you through it all. We're not just talking basics; we're going deep into each platform, understanding our audience, and crafting resonating content. And while I'm focusing on our bustling Main Street, these strategies are gold for any small business across the U.S. Ready to join the social media revolution? Let's jump in!

1. Choosing the Right Platforms for Your Business

Selecting the right social media platform is like finding the perfect location for your store – it's crucial. Let's break down the key players:

a. Facebook: Think of Facebook as the town square of social media. It's popular among a broad age group, especially those aged 30-60 and beyond. It's fantastic for detailed storytelling, sharing events, and building a community. Here, you can share longer posts, engage in conversations, and sell products directly through Facebook Marketplace. Make sure you connect with me @johntpeters.

b. Instagram: Instagram is like a trendy digital art gallery for images and content, dominated by the 18-40 age bracket. It's perfect for visually driven content. High-quality photos, stories, and short videos can truly shine here. Use it to showcase your products and offer a behind-the-scenes look into your business. This is where I've found the most success with influencer marketing. Make sure you connect with me @johntpeters.

c. X (formerly Twitter): Quick, concise, and always buzzing, Twitter appeals to a wide range, including the informed 25-50 age group. It's ideal for sharing industry news, quick updates, and engaging directly with customers through witty, timely tweets. Make sure you connect with me @johntpeters.

d. LinkedIn The professional networking hall. LinkedIn is best for B2B interactions and networking with professionals aged 25-55 (and yes, I'm over 55, but I'm young at heart and a digital native, so you'll find me there as well). It's a platform for sharing industry insights, company news, and professional content. It helps to establish yourself as a business thought leader in your specialty. I'm a big fan of LinkedIn. Make sure you connect with me @johntpeters.

e. TikTok is the new vibrant dance floor of social media, immensely popular with Gen Z and younger Millennials (ages 16-30). It's all about creativity, trends, and fun, short-form videos. This platform can offer tremendous reach if your business can create engaging and creative content.

f. Pinterest: Often overlooked, Pinterest is a visual search engine and idea board popular with women aged 25-45. It's great for businesses with visually appealing products or services, such as home decor, fashion, and food. In case you don't know, I do a lot of painting and drawing, and I use Pinterest for the art aspect of my life.

Remember, it's not about being on every platform but choosing the right ones where your target customers are most active.

2. Creating Engaging Content Strategies

Crafting content for social media is like curating a unique exhibit for your business – it needs to be thoughtful, engaging, and reflective of your brand. Let's dive deeper into developing a content strategy that captivates your audience:

1. Understanding Your Audience: You must understand your audience before creating content. What do they like? What are their interests? For example, if your Hackensack café is popular among young professionals, your content should mirror the style and tone that resonates with that demographic. Conduct surveys, read comments, and analyze engagement to understand their preferences.

2. Storytelling Through Visuals: Humans are visual creatures, and compelling images or videos can powerfully convey your brand's story. For a boutique, this might mean posting high-quality pictures of new arrivals, while a tech store could share short videos showcasing the latest gadgets. Remember Casual Habana's viral video? It succeeded because it told a relatable, engaging story. Think about what story you want to know through your visuals.

3. Leveraging Trends and Timely Content: Stay up-to-date with current trends, whether it's a viral TikTok challenge or a topical meme. Integrating these trends into your content can increase relatability and shareability. For instance, if a trending challenge fits your business persona, join in! It's about balancing being timely and staying true to your brand.

4. Educational and How-To Content: People love to learn new things, especially from experts. Share your knowledge in an accessible way. A kitchen store could post cooking tips or how-to videos on using their products. This type of content not only educates but also subtly promotes your products.

5. Interactive and Engaging Posts: Social media is a two-way street. Encourage interaction by asking questions, creating polls, or hosting Q&A sessions. For instance, a bookstore might ask followers for book recommendations. Interactive posts engage your audience and provide valuable insights into their preferences.

6. Consistent Posting Schedule: Consistency is key in social media. Create a content calendar to plan your posts. This ensures that your audience regularly hears from you, keeping your brand at the top of their minds. It doesn't mean bombarding them with daily posts but finding a rhythm that keeps your audience engaged without overwhelming them.

7. User-Generated Content and Community Building: Encourage your customers to share their experiences with your brand. User-generated content, like a customer sharing a photo of their favorite meal at your restaurant, is authentic and builds community. Reposting customer content (with permission) shows appreciation and adds credibility to your brand.

8. Diversifying Your Content Types: Don't stick to one type of content. Mix it up! If you run a gym, share motivational quotes, client testimonials, and nutrition tips alongside workout videos. Different content types keep your feed fresh and appealing.

9. Seasonal and Local Content: Tap into local events and seasons. If Hackensack is hosting a festival, align your content with it. Like a special menu item for the holiday season, seasonal posts connect your brand with the community's rhythm.

10. Behind-the-scenes and Team Highlights: People connect with people. Share behind-the-scenes glimpses of your business or highlight team members. It personalizes your brand and fosters a deeper connection with your audience.

Developing a robust content strategy involves understanding your audience, being creative and diverse in your content types, and maintaining a consistent, engaging presence. This is the perfect recipe for creating a social media presence that best represents your brand while driving loyalty and building trust in the community.

Working with Social Media Influencers

Influencers have significant followings and can promote your business for a fee. But choose wisely – relevance and engagement matter more than follower count. Here's what to consider:

1. **Relevance to the Audience:** Ensure the influencer's audience matches your target market.

2. **Engagement Rate:** Look for influencers with active, engaged followers.

3. **Authenticity and Brand Fit:** Choose influencers whose style aligns with your brand.

4. **Quality of Content:** Ensure the influencer produces consistent content.

5. **Budget and Expectations:** Be clear about your budget and what you expect from the partnership.

3. Measuring and Analyzing Social Media Impact

Introduction to Social Media Analytics: No marketing effort is complete without analytics. Here's what to track concerning social media:

• **Engagement Metrics:** Monitor likes, comments, shares, and views. These indicate how well your content resonates with your audience.

• **Follower Growth:** A steady increase in followers suggests your content is appealing and reaching new audiences.

• **Website Traffic:** Use tools like Google Analytics to track if your social media efforts drive traffic to your website.

• **Conversion Rates:** Ultimately, we're here to grow our businesses. Track how many of these interactions turn into actual sales or leads.

AI Topic: Using AI in Social Media for Small Business:

In the bustling world of social media, where every like, share, and comment counts, AI is a game-changer for small businesses like ours (and yours) on Main Street.

Picture this: you're running a cozy café or a trendy boutique and have a ton on your plate. AI is your digital helper, smartly sorting through heaps of online data to understand what your customers love. It's like having a savvy assistant who knows which pastry picture or fashion post will likely bring more folks through your door. AI tools analyze patterns in customer interactions, helping you tailor your posts to catch the eye of your target audience at the right time. So, whether you're showcasing a new line of earrings or the daily special at your café, AI helps ensure your content resonates with your followers, increasing engagement without you having to dive into the nitty-gritty of data analysis.

But wait, there's more to AI than just data crunching. It's also about conversations and relationships. Think of AI as the friendly neighborhood robot that never sleeps and is always ready to chat with your customers. Using AI-powered chatbots on your social media platforms, you can instantly respond to customer inquiries about your latest tech gadgets or book an appointment at your salon. These chatbots are programmed to understand and respond to common queries, providing your customers with a seamless and interactive experience. This means better customer service without you being glued to your screen. In essence,

AI in social media is about smarter marketing, personalized customer experiences, and freeing up valuable time – a trio that can make a real difference for small businesses thriving on Main Street, across Hackensack, and beyond.

Conclusion: Crafting Your Social Media Saga

And there you have it – a deep dive into making social media work for your small business. We've covered choosing the right platforms, crafting engaging content, and understanding the importance of analytics. Remember, social media marketing is an ongoing connecting, engaging, and growing journey. It's about authenticity and finding the right mix that resonates with your audience and reflects your business.

CHAPTER 15: MOBILE MARKETING ON MAIN STREET USA

Summary and Introduction: Reaching Mobile Users

Mobile marketing, a pivotal aspect of community and small business marketing strategies nationwide, offers opportunities. In the past, individuals would plan their local outings from the comfort of their homes, searching for information about nearby downtown shopping or entertainment districts. However, the landscape has drastically changed. Today, these same individuals are already in our communities, strolling down Main Street and using their smartphones to access the information they need, all at their fingertips. This shift in consumer behavior presents a unique chance for small businesses to reach a vast mobile audience and secure their share of the seemingly infinite mobile information space.

With this significant shift in consumer behavior, communities and small businesses must adapt and compete for the attention of this vast mobile audience. They must strive to secure their share of the seemingly infinite mobile information space.

Starting Point: Checking Your Online Visibility

A practical starting point for small businesses is to assess their online visibility. Conduct a straightforward Google search using your town's official name, business name, or main category. For instance, if you operate a jewelry store, search for "Hackensack Jewelry Store" and review the results. If your listing doesn't appear in the top three results, it's time to investigate those that do. Remember, if your business isn't on the first page, it's as good as non-existent online.

Google Maps

Maintaining accurate, up-to-date information about your business on Google should always be a top priority. Google has transitioned from Google My Business to integrating business profiles into Google Maps. By finding your business through Google search or maps, you can take control of your profile and ensure the information is complete and current. Google offers a Profile Strength Indicator, which helps measure how thorough your business information is.

Directory Sites

Investing time and some ad dollars in directory sites can benefit small businesses. Numerous community and business directory listing and review sites exist, with some of the best-known being Yelp, TripAdvisor, Nextdoor for Business, and the

Yellow Pages. Yelp, in particular, offers great resources for small businesses. All of these directories provide various paid advertising and promotion options.

Mobile Apps

The phrase "There's an app for that!" is well-known, and mobile applications have gained significant popularity for specific areas of interest. Some communities may need to create their own mobile app, which initially sounds logical. A standalone, community-specific mobile app could include all the information a visitor would need: a map, parking info, local attractions, business directory, events calendar, etc. However, this approach has several issues.

The main problem is that the only people who will download such an app are the locals, who already know where things are and don't need directions or information about local businesses. Additionally, marketing the app to people outside the community is challenging and costly. Without substantial regional or national advertising budgets, reaching potential visitors from nearby towns or farther away is difficult.

Furthermore, developing a quality, user-friendly app is expensive. Professional apps can cost anywhere from $25,000 to $50,000 or more. After development, maintaining and updating the app, distributing it through the Apple and Google app stores, and then marketing it to ensure downloads are daunting.

An Alternative Solution

Instead of creating a new app, consider using a solution like Distrx, which is now part of Locable. Distrx is a location-aware mobile app with hundreds of communities and businesses nationwide. The app provides content based on the user's current location, making it a comprehensive resource for all communities. It features a community map with parking locations and area attractions, a business directory by category, and an events calendar. Businesses can create and control their listings and post promotions. The app is free for communities and local businesses, with the company generating revenue from paid options such as walking tours, interactive scavenger hunts, and other app-based activities. Using Distrx, you can foster a sense of community and connection, making users feel more engaged with their local businesses and attractions and, ultimately, driving more traffic to your business.

So, if you're a business in Hackensack, download the Distrx app, search for "Downtown Hackensack," find your business listing, claim it, and start promoting your business effectively.

CHAPTER 16:
REACHING THE NEW RESIDENTS

Summary and Introduction: Reaching Out Via Community Engagement

We've spent much time discussing how to engage with the community, but a specific group needs a dedicated strategy: new residents. In this crucial chapter, we'll explore how to weave our businesses into the very fabric of our local community, focusing specifically on newcomers. These new residents aren't just potential customers but future advocates and key to your business's growth. They chose our city for various reasons—perhaps a beautiful, affordable apartment or proximity to a new job. Regardless of why they're here, they likely don't appreciate the incredible transformation Hackensack has undergone over the years. They only see the present, and we must ensure it's shining bright for them and all our residents. Engaging with new residents is about attracting new customers, building a loyal customer base, and fostering a sense of community.

Where to Start: Welcoming New Residents

The most important thing to do with a new resident is to welcome them with open arms. Let's explore how we can make our businesses a welcoming beacon for these individuals.

Identifying New Residents

Identifying new residents in our community is like finding hidden treasures. They're eager to explore and connect with their new surroundings. Here are some strategies to tap into this demographic:

Partner with Real Estate Agents: I regularly chat with local real estate brokers and property managers from new buildings. We have a new program launching soon called "Welcome to Main Street!" Through this program, we'll provide welcome packages encouraging new residents to download our app, which features special offers from local businesses. If you've claimed your business on the Downtown Hackensack app, you can include your promotions there. This program introduces the MSBA and all our member businesses to newcomers as they set up their new lives. If you want to be part of this initiative, please reach out to us.

Social Media Monitoring: Monitor local social media groups for mentions of new moves. A friendly welcome message can go a long way. For example, if someone posts, "Just moved into town. Where's a good place to get a pizza?" Someone from Mob

Pizza and Burgers should respond with, "Come on down. We've got fresh pies in the oven!" (If you're reading this in the Midwest, "pies" refers to pizza pies, not your apple and pumpkin varieties.)

Referral Benefits: Offer a referral discount to encourage existing customers to bring in new residents. This will turn your current customers into active promoters of your business.

Hosting Community Welcome Events

Hosting or participating in welcome events can significantly boost your visibility among new residents:

Organize Meet-and-Greets: We're working with a few business owners to host casual meet-and-greet events in their stores, inviting locals and new residents. It's a relaxed way for newcomers to mingle and learn about local businesses.

Participate in Community Events: Joining community events like fairs or festivals is an excellent way to reach new residents. Setting up a booth or sponsoring a part of the event can draw attention to your business.

Collaborating with Local Businesses and Organizations

Unity is strength! Collaborating with fellow local businesses can create a support network for new residents. Roberto from SUNMED has fantastic ideas about how local companies could partner through collaborations and cross-promotions. Ask him to tell you about what he did for the two months BEFORE he opened his store. He and his wife, Toni, walked all around Hackensack handing out cards and meeting almost every business owner or manager, all to introduce themselves and their business.

Utilizing Social Media for Local Engagement

Social media isn't just a global tool; it's incredibly powerful for local engagement:

Welcome Posts: Regularly post welcome messages on your social media, using local hashtags to attract new residents.

Showcasing Community Involvement: Share posts about local events or causes your business supports. This demonstrates your commitment to the community, resonating with newcomers looking to connect with socially responsible businesses.

Creating Content That Resonates with Newcomers

Craft content that answers the typical queries of someone new to the area:

Local Guides: Share local guides like "Top 10 Places to Visit in Hackensack." Who writes these guides? Well, we do, but you can too. At the least, you could create posts and refer to the MSBA guides on our website. These guides provide valuable information to new residents and position the MSBA as a community expert and sharing them confirms you're "in the know" regarding community information. This is one of the most important content-generation tasks.

Settling-In Tips: Posts offering tips for new residents, like where to find local amenities, can be incredibly helpful and build goodwill. Creating this content also lets you showcase your business and those you collaborate with. Coordinate posting schedules with your partners for maximum impact.

Engaging with Local Community Groups and Forums

Make it a point to be active in local community groups and online forums:

Answering Questions: Jump in to answer queries from new residents. Direct engagement positions your business as helpful and approachable. Sharing your expertise without overt selling builds credibility and subtly promotes your business.

Feedback Loop with New Customers

Feedback is golden. Always seek new residents' opinions and experiences:

Casual Conversations: Post-visit casual conversations can provide insights into what new residents are looking for and how you can better cater to their needs. Building strong relationships with new residents can turn them into loyal customers.

Conclusion: Fostering Long-Term Relationships

Engaging new residents isn't just a one-off strategy; it's about fostering long-term relationships. Integrating these approaches into your business model creates a welcoming atmosphere for newcomers and lays the foundation for lasting customer loyalty. Remember, each new resident you impress today can become a loyal advocate for your business tomorrow. Let's make our mark on Hackensack's community and grow together! If your business is in another city, engaging with new residents is a great way to launch your business.

CHAPTER 17: LEVERAGING AI IN SMALL BUSINESS MARKETING FOR ENTREPRENEURS

Summary and Introduction to AI in Marketing

Let me start by saying, while I personally have tried dozens of AI tools for all types of uses, I believe you really don't need more than a few to run your small business, and in total, they shouldn't cost more than $60 per month. I'm talking about straight AI tools, not tools which include AI functionality. So, what are the three I think you need? ChatGPT, Claude, and Gemini. I know a bunch of folks who swear by Jasper, but I find those are the people who struggled with AI prompts early on and Jasper is good at holding your hand. I list a bunch more in the resources section of this book, but I'd start with these three. Four if you nee prompt help and want to use Jasper. You'll end up cutting this list down after a couple weeks of using them. But you should use them. Why? In today's digital age, Artificial Intelligence (AI) and Generative AI (GenAI) are more than just buzzwords; they're game-changers for marketing strategies, especially for small businesses everywhere. AI involves computers performing tasks that typically require human intelligence—like learning from data, making decisions, and automating repetitive tasks. Its transformative power in marketing lies in its ability to process and analyze vast amounts of data, providing insights and automation that were previously out of reach due to cost or complexity.

For small business owners, embracing AI is about recognizing its potential to level the playing field. AI offers smaller enterprises personalized insights into customer behavior, enhances customer interactions, and automates routine tasks, freeing owners to focus on core business activities. AI in marketing augments human creativity and decision-making with data-driven insights. Techniques like machine learning analyze large datasets to identify patterns and trends in consumer behavior. For instance, AI can evaluate customer purchase history to predict future buying habits, enabling businesses to tailor their marketing strategies more effectively and personally.

Addressing Local Marketing Challenges with AI

The local business landscape presents unique marketing challenges, from attracting new customers to growing a social media presence. Let's delve into how AI can address these issues.

Attracting New Customers with AI: AI tools excel in identifying potential new customers, especially those new to the neighborhood. By analyzing geolocation data and social media trends, AI helps businesses target their marketing efforts more effectively. For example, an AI system can scan local online forums and social media posts to identify newcomers to your city, allowing you to direct targeted marketing campaigns to these individuals.

Enhancing Social Media Presence through AI: Social media platforms are treasure troves of user data. AI-driven analytics can optimize a business's social media strategy by analyzing patterns in user interactions. AI algorithms can suggest the most engaging types of content, the best times for posting, and effective engagement tactics. This means businesses can grow their following more efficiently and increase engagement on platforms like Facebook, Instagram, and Twitter.

AI Tools for Marketing

Various AI tools have emerged to cater to different aspects of marketing, providing small businesses with powerful capabilities:

ChatGPT in Marketing: This GenAI tool is revolutionizing content creation and customer service for small businesses. ChatGPT can assist in drafting emails, creating engaging blog posts, scripting video content, and even generating creative marketing campaign ideas. Its integration into customer service platforms provides instant, accurate responses to customer inquiries, which is invaluable for after-hours queries.

Jasper for Content Creation: Jasper is designed to ease the burden of content creation. It can generate marketing copy, blog posts, and social media content, helping overcome writer's block by providing sample sentences and paragraphs. It also suggests content ideas tailored to the latest trends and business needs.

Lavender.ai: Lavender.ai analyzes what's working in your sales and marketing emails and provides feedback for improvements. They call themselves an "email intelligence company with an AI email coach." This tool is invaluable for refining email communication strategies.

Canva's AI-Enhanced Design: Known for its design capabilities, Canva has integrated AI to aid businesses in creating visually appealing designs. Its AI suggests layouts, color palettes, and branding elements, making it an invaluable tool for maintaining brand consistency.

Other Essential AI Tools: HubSpot offers comprehensive CRM and marketing automation with AI capabilities. Hootsuite's AI-powered social media management tools streamline posting and engagement strategies. SEMrush provides AI-driven SEO insights, helping businesses improve their online visibility.

Practical Applications Across Business Types

AI and GenAI can be applied across various types of businesses, each benefiting in unique ways:

Cafés and Restaurants: AI can personalize marketing efforts based on customer preferences and dining habits. It can suggest menu adjustments based on trend analysis and manage efficient online reservation systems.

Tech Shops: AI assists in inventory management by predicting trends and customer preferences. It can also enhance customer recommendations based on past purchases and automate after-sales service communications.

Legal Firms: AI streamlines appointment scheduling and enhances client relationship management. It provides data-driven insights for better market positioning and client retention strategies.

Nail Salons and Barber Shops use AI tools to schedule appointments efficiently, analyze popular styles or treatment trends, and create targeted local advertising campaigns to attract nearby clientele.

An Overview of Using AI Tools

Implementing AI in business operations requires a strategic approach:

Personalized Marketing with AI: Collect customer data from various sources, such as website interactions, social media activity, and purchase history. AI tools will analyze this data, identifying customer behavior and preference patterns. Segment your customers into groups based on common characteristics like demographics, buying behavior, and engagement levels. Create marketing campaigns tailored to each segment, leveraging AI's predictive analytics to anticipate future customer behavior. This can guide inventory management, promotional offers, and product development.

AI for Social Media Strategy: Use AI to understand better your audience's interests, behaviors, and engagement patterns. Determine the most effective types of content for your audience, including format, tone, and subject matter. AI tools can suggest the best times for posting based on peak audience activity and automate the posting process for consistency. Employ AI to analyze the performance of your social media campaigns, measuring engagement rates, reach, and effectiveness of different content types.

Understanding AI Mechanics

To effectively leverage AI, you need to understand the basics. Machines use algorithms to learn from data, identify patterns, and make decisions with minimal human involvement. Natural language processing enables AI and GenAI to understand and generate human-like text, crucial for tools like ChatGPT in content creation and customer service.

Ethical and Legal Considerations in AI and GenAI

Ethical and legal considerations are crucial when implementing AI in marketing. Establishing strict data privacy and security protocols is essential, as well as ensuring compliance with regulations like GDPR (European Union's General Data Protection Regulation) and CCPA (California Consumer Privacy Act). Transparency with customers about how their data is used in AI-driven marketing is vital, including obtaining consent where necessary. Regularly auditing AI algorithms to avoid biases and stereotypes is also important to maintain fairness and avoid alienating segments of your customer base. Stay informed on AI regulations by consulting with AI and data privacy experts to ensure your marketing practices remain compliant and ethical. If this feels overwhelming, remember that AI is here to stay, and getting up to speed quickly is essential.

The Ever-Evolving Landscape of AI in Marketing

AI technology is evolving rapidly, making it crucial for small businesses to stay informed and adaptable. There is no doubt in my mind that by the time you read this, the AI/GenAI sections will require updating. So don't stop learning. Continuous learning about new AI technologies and techniques will benefit you and enhance your marketing efforts. Develop marketing strategies that are flexible enough to incorporate new AI technologies as they emerge. While there may be some initial investments, they are minimal compared to the long-term benefits. Embrace AI solutions that allow your marketing efforts to grow and make your operations more efficient.

Integrating AI with Traditional Marketing Content

Creating a balanced marketing strategy involves blending AI insights with traditional marketing intuition. Use AI for data-driven decisions while retaining the human element in customer relationships and brand storytelling. Ensure that AI-enhanced strategies do not overlook the importance of local community engagement and personal customer service. Balance AI efficiency with a human touch in your marketing to maintain authenticity and personal connections.

Practical Examples of Using AI Daily

Here are six ways I or some of my associates use AI and GenAI daily:

1. **Morning Analysis with AI Analytics Tool:** Using Google Analytics with AI Insights to review website traffic and visitor behavior, saving an hour or two each week on data analysis.

2. **Automated Email Sorting with an AI Email Assistant:** Testing SaneBox, an AI email management tool, to prioritize and sort emails, potentially saving an hour a week.

3. **Customer Service with AI Chatbots:** Using tools like Intercom or Drift to handle basic customer queries, saving several hours daily instantly.

4. **Social Media Bulk Content Creation with GenAI & Graphics Platform:** Using ChatGPT and Canva to create 100 social media posts with graphics in 15 minutes, saving many hours. The first time I successfully managed to do this absolutely blew my mind.

5. **Social Media Management with AI Scheduler:** Use Hootsuite's AI capabilities to schedule and optimize posts, saving around an hour daily.

6. **Financial Insights with AI Accounting Software:** Using QuickBooks Online with AI-driven insights for real-time financial health insights, saving around an hour per week.

Conclusion: Navigating the AI Landscape

While this chapter aims to provide small business owners with valuable insights into leveraging AI and GenAI in marketing, it's important to recognize that AI is advancing incredibly. This guide will empower local businesses with the knowledge and tools to effectively integrate AI into their marketing strategies, ensuring they remain competitive and innovative in a rapidly changing digital world. Keep AI at the forefront of your mind, continuously learn and adapt, and always balance AI efficiency with a human touch to create authentic and engaging marketing experiences.

CHAPTER 18: SUSTAINING BUSINESS GROWTH AND INNOVATION

Summary and Introduction

We've been talking a lot about growth in this book, haven't we? But now, let's shift gears and focus on keeping that growth going strong. While we might cover some familiar ground, some subtle differences are worth exploring.

Cultivating Innovation

Every small business holds the potential for big ideas, whether you're a dynamic duo or a team of twenty. Some folks seem to have a knack for turning ideas into action. So, let's chat about how to bring those brilliant ideas to life, which is the important part.

Hold Innovation Sessions: These aren't your run-of-the-mill meetings. Think of them as creativity boot camps, where you and your team can play with ideas without limitations. I even suggest bringing in fresh perspectives from customers or local students. As part of a capstone project, I recently pitched some challenges to students at Fairleigh Dickinson University, and boy, they delivered some amazing ideas!

These virtual or in-person sessions should be safe spaces where every idea can shine. It's like a brainstorming party where everyone's invited, including those outsiders you brought in. During these meetings, it's crucial not to shoot down any ideas. Do you know what's worse than saying no? That dreaded phrase: "But we've tried that before." Just because something didn't work in the past doesn't mean it won't work now. Also, if you say "We've tried that before…" you assuming you did it correctly and who says you did? So, let everyone speak up next time you're brainstorming and work through their ideas. Encourage voices to be heard. You'll be amazed at how engaged your team becomes.

Lifelong Learning as Your Business's Backbone

I can't tell you how often I've spoken to business owners who say, "Business has slowed, but we're sticking to what we've always done." Well, guess what? The world keeps spinning, and so should you. That's why fostering a culture of continuous learning within your company is crucial. You've got to be willing to take risks and encourage your team to try new things.

Tailored Learning Journeys: Everyone's got their strengths and interests. Develop individual learning plans that help your team members grow in their chosen directions. You can align their personal growth with your business's needs when done right. Remember that person who said, "That's something only big companies do," then called me looking for job referrals? If you had given your employees a chance to learn and grow, they probably wouldn't have left. Learning doesn't have to be complex; it can be as simple as having a monthly coffee chat with your team where they can ask you anything. Believe me, most people just want the opportunity to learn.

Weekly Wisdom Exchanges: Set aside time each week for team members to share something new they've learned. It could be a tech tip, a customer service insight, or an industry trend. Make it enjoyable, like a mini-TED Talk during lunch. I once attended such a meeting at a restaurant, and a waitstaff member shared a time-saving trick for looking up reservations. Two other staff members immediately said, "That's genius!"

Smart Growth Strategies

If you've taken the plunge and implemented some of the ideas from this book, you know that growth is thrilling. Now, let's make sure it's sustainable. We're not just growing; we're growing smarter.

Readiness Check: Before you leap, take a good look around. If you're about to implement something to spur growth, assess your business's capacity first. Are you ready? Can your current systems handle more customers? Is your team prepared for growth? This is about scaling up while maintaining what makes your small business special.

Staying True to Your Roots: As you grow, don't lose sight of what makes your small business unique. Remember, those personal touches, that sense of community, and genuine customer care set you apart. If you lose any of these things, you're not headed down the right path.

Conclusion: Sustain Your Growth

By now, you might feel like you've been on a deep dive into the sea of growth and innovation. If there's one thing you should take away from this, keeping your business alive is just the beginning. It would be best to have a vibrant, always-evolving business full of innovation. Hopefully, you'll foster an environment where your employees constantly learn something new. Think of this as a friendly push to keep pushing forward, dream big, and never settle for "good enough." Sustaining growth is about keeping that spark of creativity, curiosity, and daring moves alive and well. If you've heard me say it once, you've heard me say it a thousand times: "Forward Always!" Sure, it's okay to sidestep occasionally, but always capitalize on that momentum.

CHAPTER 19:
DEEPENING YOUR SMALL BUSINESS'S COMMUNITY ROOTS

Building Bonds Beyond Business – The B4 Strategy

Your business is more than just a place for transactions; it should be a cornerstone in your community. Let's explore how you can strengthen the ties between you, your business, and your community.

Active Community Engagement: If you're wondering why this subject keeps coming up in this book, it's because this is critically important. Not kind of important. Not very important. CRITICALLY important. I'll say it again; people do business with people, not companies. Be visible and active in your community. Sponsor a little league team, host workshops, or organize clean-up events. It's about showing up and making a difference, not just for your business but also for your neighbors.

Partnerships That Matter: Join forces with local non-profits, schools, and other businesses for causes that resonate with you. Whether it's a fundraiser for the local animal shelter or a back-to-school drive, these collaborations amplify your impact and foster lasting relationships.

Championing Sustainability and Social Responsibility

Making a positive impact in sustainability is an integral part of doing business. Here's how you can contribute:

Sustainability in Action: Take stock of your sustainability practices. Small changes like reducing paper use or supporting local suppliers can make a big difference. Share your sustainability journey with your community to inspire others to follow suit. Don't hesitate to seek input from others on how they're improving sustainability practices, too.

Giving Back: Find creative ways to give back to your community. Offer your space for meetings, mentor local students, or donate some of your sales to a local charity. You'll strengthen community bonds by leveraging your resources for the greater good while making a difference.

Using Technology to Bring People Together – There's an App for That

In today's digital age, technology can help strengthen community ties. Here's how:

Community Apps: Support apps that serve your community, such as Downtown Hackensack by Distrx, which is geo-location based wo wherever in the US you go, the app find the closest community to where you are. These platforms allow local businesses to offer exclusive deals and share updates. Additionally, consider creating a community Facebook page to facilitate communication and connection.

Data for Good: Understand your community's needs and preferences using data analytics. This goes beyond targeting ads; it's about genuinely understanding your community's values and how your business can contribute to its well-being. If your company is within a Special Improvement District (SID) or Business Improvement District (BID), leverage their data to address community preferences.

Conclusion: Strengthening Your Ties Within the Community

Growing and innovating as a small business means embracing change, nurturing creativity, and forging authentic connections with your community. The key word here is "authentic." It's about using technology not only to sell but to serve and scale your business for profit and purpose. Strive to be the small business your community is proud of today and in the future.

THE FINAL CONCLUSION:
EMBRACING YOUR BUSINESS JOURNEY ON MAIN STREET

Well, that's a wrap. Or is it? As we reach the end of this guide, you should realize that your journey is about to begin. So, first, I want to take a moment to commend you for embarking on this journey of discovery and growth for your business. The path of an entrepreneur is filled with challenges and rewards, and your dedication to enhancing your business knowledge, particularly in marketing and strategic planning, is a testament to your commitment to success.

Throughout this book, we have navigated various facets of marketing and business development, each chapter providing insights and practical strategies tailored for the unique landscape of Hackensack's Main Street. From understanding your market to embracing the latest trends in digital marketing, from the power of networking to the potential of strategic partnerships, and from the importance of budgeting to the exciting world of business grants, we've covered a broad spectrum of tools and techniques to help your business thrive.

Remember, the journey does not end here. The business world is dynamic, constantly evolving with new trends, technologies, and customer expectations. Your willingness to adapt, learn, and grow is the key to continued success. Embrace the changes, for they bring opportunities to innovate and stand out in a competitive market.

As the Executive Director of the Main Street Business Alliance, I want to assure you that you are not alone in this journey. Our alliance is, and I am, here to support, guide, and provide you with the resources needed to navigate the complexities of running a business. Whether through workshops, one-on-one consultations, or networking events, we are committed to your growth and success.

In closing, I encourage you to revisit the chapters of this book as you continue to grow your business. The strategies and insights provided here are meant to be your companions as you face the exciting challenges of entrepreneurship. So please don't hesitate to contact the Main Street Business Alliance for support and guidance or share your successes and challenges.

Your business is vital to the Hackensack community, contributing economically, culturally, and socially. Each step you take towards growth and improvement reverberates through our community, making Main Street not just a location but a vibrant hub of innovation, collaboration, and success.

Thank you for your dedication, passion, and commitment to excellence. Here's to your continued success and the bright future of Main Street, Hackensack!

Wishing you all the best in your business endeavors,

John T. Peters
Executive Director
Main Street Business Alliance

CHECKLISTS

The following are checklists for each chapter. I've put them all in one place so you better understand the entire process.

CHAPTER 1: UNDERSTANDING YOUR MARKET:

Demographics Understanding:
- Access US Census data.
- Identify key demographic insights.

Engagement Strategies:
- Host community events.
- Share business history.
- Implement loyalty programs.

Connecting with New Residents:
- Implement online ordering.
- Utilize social media.
- Ensure business listing on local apps.

Local Market Trends:
- Introduce health-conscious options.
- Host related events or workshops.

Competitive Analysis:
- Visit and observe competitors.
- Identify gaps and innovate.

Engagement with New Residents:
- Collaborate with apartments.
- Provide welcome packages.

AI for Predictive Analytics:
- Consider AI implementation.
- Analyze trends and patterns.

Conclusion:
- Tailor strategies to community needs.

CHAPTER 2: BRANDING YOUR BUSINESS

1. Understanding Branding Essence:
- Define core values and unique experiences.
- Create a brand personality that aligns with your business.

2. Visual Identity:
- Design a logo that is simple, memorable, and versatile.
- Choose a color scheme that reflects your brand's personality.

3. Developing Brand Message:
- Craft a clear and consistent brand message.
- Implement the message across all customer touchpoints.

4. Evolving and Refreshing Brand:
- Conduct periodic brand audits.
- Refresh brand elements if needed while staying aligned with core values.

5. Engaging Your Audience:
- Share your brand story through various channels.
- Participate in community events to reinforce brand presence.

6. Leveraging Local Culture:
- Embrace local themes, traditions, and trends in branding.
- Collaborate with local businesses or artists to create unique experiences.

7. AI-Driven Brand Analysis:
- Utilize AI tools to analyze brand elements and customer responses.
- Adapt branding strategies based on AI insights.

8. Case Studies:
- Study hypothetical success stories for inspiration and insights.

9. Conclusion:
- Remember that your brand is your handshake, story, and promise to customers.
- Continuously align your brand with customer needs and aspirations.

CHAPTER 3: DIGITAL MARKETING ESSENTIALS FOR SMALL BUSINESSES

1. Building a Robust Online Presence:
- Create a user-friendly website with essential information.
- Optimize for local SEO to improve visibility in search results.
- Encourage and facilitate customer reviews.

2. Content Marketing: Telling Your Story Online:
- Share relevant and engaging content on your website and social media.
- Utilize blog posts, articles, and visual content to showcase your brand.

3. Leveraging Social Media for Engagement:
- Choose the right platforms based on your target audience.
- Post regularly and interact with your followers.

- Consider outsourcing social media management if necessary.

4. Social Media Influencers:
- Choose influencers relevant to your brand and audience.
- Assess engagement rates, authenticity, and brand fit before collaborating.
- Set clear objectives and expectations for influencer partnerships.

5. Email Marketing: Direct Connection with Customers:
- Build an email list by offering incentives for signups. Most website builders like WordPress and Wix have email plug-ins so you don't need to do any programming or anything special other than install the plugin on your homepage.
- Craft personalized newsletters with relevant content and offers.
- Utilize email marketing tools like Constant Contact or MailChimp to manage your email lists and send these newsletters.
- Don't over-email your list because email fatigue will happen, and people will unsubscribe.
- Keep your newsletter balanced with useful information, special offers, and entertaining content.
- Track open rates and unsubscribed accounts.

6. Using AI in Personalized Marketing:
- Implement AI tools to segment your audience and personalize marketing efforts.
- Utilize tools like Lavender.ai for email marketing optimization and feedback.

7. Conclusion:
- Embrace digital marketing as a necessity in today's business landscape.
- Connect, engage, and convert online audiences into loyal customers.
- Transform your business by leveraging the digital realm effectively.

CHAPTER 4: LOCAL OUTREACH AND NETWORKING

1. The Value of Community Engagement:
- Participate in local events and support community causes.
- Build brand awareness locally by engaging with the community.

2. Making the Most of Local Events:
- Participate in or host events like street fairs and festivals.
- Check local event listings and collaborate with community organizations.

3. Strategic Collaborations with Other Businesses:
- Identify complementary businesses for joint promotions.
- Collaborate on events or promotions to expand marketing reach.

4. Utilizing Local Media:
- Share business news and events through press releases and local advertising.
- Get involved in community features in newspapers, blogs, and podcasts.

5. Networking for Business Growth:
- Join business networking groups, workshops, and seminars.
- Connect with other local entrepreneurs and professionals to explore opportunities.

6. Using AI to Best Take Advantage of Local Events:
- Leverage AI to analyze community engagement patterns and preferences.
- Personalize marketing strategies for local events based on AI insights.
- Analyze customer feedback and social media engagement post-event for refinement.

7. Conclusion:
- Participate in the community to become a recognized and respected local business.
- Every interaction and collaboration deepens your connection to the community, fostering long-term success.

CHAPTER 5: Customer Relationship Management for Small Business

1. Understanding the Fundamentals of CRM:
- CRM is crucial for fostering lasting relationships with customers.
- CRM involves systematically handling interactions and data throughout the customer journey.

2. Building a Robust Customer Database:
- Collect customer data through various touchpoints like loyalty and newsletter signups or purchases.
- Maintain transparency and privacy to build trust with customers.

3. Enhancing the Customer Experience through Personalization:
- Segment customers based on behavior, preferences, or demographics.
- Customize interactions and offers to make customers feel valued.

4. Implementing Effective Loyalty Programs:
- Design simple loyalty programs that reward repeat business.
- Promote the program across different channels to increase participation.

5. Utilizing CRM Tools for Analytics and Insights:
- Choose a CRM tool tailored to your business needs.
- Use customer data insights to inform marketing strategies and product improvements.

6. Using AI to Build Customer Loyalty:
- AI can enhance loyalty programs by personalizing rewards and predicting customer behavior.

7. Conclusion:
- CRM isn't just a strategy and a business philosophy in Hackensack.
- Embrace CRM to deepen customer relationships and contribute positively to the community.

CHAPTER 6: ANALYTICS AND MEASURING SUCCESS

1. The Value of Community Engagement:
- Being involved in the community goes beyond just business; it's about building relationships.
- Engage in local events and support causes to show your commitment to the community.

2. Making the Most of Local Events:
- Participate in or host events to showcase your business's personality and connect with the audience.
- Check local event listings and collaborate with organizations like the Main Street Business Alliance.

3. Strategic Collaborations with Other Businesses:
- Partner with complementary businesses to create joint promotions or events.
- Identify potential partners and leverage each other's strengths for mutual benefit.

4. Utilizing Local Media:
- Utilize traditional media channels like newspapers and community blogs to reach residents.
- Share news about your business and get involved in community features to increase visibility.

5. Networking for Business Growth:
- Attend networking events and workshops to connect with other local entrepreneurs.
- Join business groups like the Main Street Business Alliance or the Chamber of Commerce to expand your network.

6. Using AI to Best Take Advantage of Local Events:
- AI can analyze community engagement patterns and preferences to identify impactful events.
- Personalize marketing strategies for local events to maximize engagement and analyze feedback for future improvements.

7. Conclusion:
- Active participation in the community sets the stage for long-term business success.
- Every interaction and collaboration strengthens your business's connection with the community, contributing to its vibrant social fabric.

CHAPTER 7: BUDGETING AND RESOURCE ALLOCATION FOR SMALL BUSINESSES ON MAIN STREET

1. Crafting a Realistic Marketing Budget:
- Establish a structured marketing budget to balance business objectives with financial constraints.
- Allocate a percentage of total revenue (typically 510%) for marketing activities.
- Prioritize marketing expenditures based on potential return on investment, considering local advertising, social media, and community engagement.

2. Maximizing Your Marketing Impact with Limited Resources:
- Utilize low-cost digital tools like social media, email marketing, and basic SEO techniques.
- Engage in community-based marketing through local events, networking, and word-of-mouth referrals.
- Navigate digital marketing costs by budgeting for online advertising, website maintenance, and SEO.

3. Balancing Between Short-term and Long-term Investments:
- Distinguish between short-term tactics (e.g., seasonal promotions) and long-term strategies (e.g., brand cultivation, SEO).
- Allocate a portion of the budget for sustained growth and enduring market presence.

4. Tracking and Adjusting Your Marketing Budget:
- Monitor marketing expenses and outcomes to make informed spending adjustments.
- Remain flexible to recalibrate the budget in response to changing market dynamics and emerging opportunities.

5. Budgeting Success Stories in Hackensack:
- Draw inspiration from local businessethat achieved success through strategic budget allocation.

6. Utilizing AI to Optimize Your Budget:
- AI revolutionizes resource allocation by predicting demand, analyzing sales data, and providing insights into customer spending patterns.
- AI-driven tools can help tailor inventory and marketing efforts for maximum effectiveness.

7. Conclusion:
- Effective budgeting and resource allocation are essential for sustained growth and success on Main Street.
- Adopt a thoughtful approach to marketing spending to make informed financial decisions aligned with business goals and financial capabilities.

CHAPTER 8: STRATEGIC PARTNERSHIPS AND COLLABORATIONS

1. The Power of Strategic Partnerships:
- Partnerships extend business capabilities, reaching new customer segments and sharing marketing burdens.
- Identify potential partners aligned with your values and offerings, like a café partnering with a bookstore for joint events.

2. Crafting Mutually Beneficial Partnerships:
- Define partnership goals such as increased sales or market exposure.
- Structure collaborations through joint events, cross promotions, or shared loyalty programs.
- Sustain partnerships through effective communication, regular check-ins, and conflict resolution.

3. Local Collaborations for Community Engagement:
- Engage in initiatives that resonate with your city's identity, like participating in local festivals.
- Capitalize on local events for joint promotions, amplifying outreach and visibility.

4. Success Stories:
- Highlight local successes such as themed events at an Italian restaurant or a fashion tech fusion event.

5. AI Topic: Using AI to Find and Nurture Partnerships:
- AI can revolutionize partnership identification and management, optimizing outcomes and decisions. With a little of learning, AI will open up a new world for you to easily gather information.

6. Conclusion:
- Embrace strategic partnerships to enrich potential, foster innovation, and deepen community engagement in today's dynamic business landscape.

CHAPTER 9: SEEING THE PATH FORWARD TO NAVIGATE THE EVER-CHANGING LANDSCAPE OF MARKETING

Incorporating Augmented Reality (AR) in Marketing:
- AR enhances customer engagement with virtual try-ons and product visualization.
- Identify opportunities and develop immersive AR experiences that add value to the customer journey.

Implementing Eco-Friendly Marketing Initiatives:
- Audit practices and communicate sustainability efforts transparently to customers.
- Host sustainable events and collaborate with like-minded businesses to amplify the message.

Personalized Marketing Using Data Analytics:
- Collect and utilize customer data to tailor marketing campaigns for deeper engagement.
- Segment the audience based on preferences and behaviors to create personalized experiences.

Effective Use of Influencer Marketing:
- Identify relevant influencers aligned with the target demographic.
- Establish clear collaborations, set goals, and measure the impact of influencer campaigns for maximum ROI.

Adapting to Market Changes with Agile Marketing:
- Stay informed on market trends through various sources and attend workshops.
- Implement flexible marketing strategies that allow for quick response and experimentation.

How AI Might Help with Marketing:
- AI provides insights into predicting and adapting to future marketing trends.
- Analyze digital trends and predict consumer behaviors to remain competitive.

CHAPTER 10: GRANTS AND FUNDING OPPORTUNITIES FOR BUSINESSES

1. Understanding the Landscape of Business Grants:
- Identify different types of grants: federal, state, local, and private.
- Research grants using online databases, government websites, and business associations.

2. The Grant Application Process: A Step-by-Step Guide:
- Prepare necessary documents: business plans, financial statements, tax returns, etc.
- Understand grant requirements, including business size, industry niche, and fund usage.
- Write a compelling grant proposal with an executive summary, project plans, and a clear budget.

3. Utilizing Local and State Grants:
- Explore resources from local organizations like the Main Street Business Alliance and Bergen County Department of Economic Development.
- Highlight community impact in grant applications, showcasing how your business contributes to Hackensack's wellbeing.

4. Effectively Managing Grant Funds:
- Set up a tracking system to monitor fund utilization and ensure alignment with proposed objectives.
- Adhere to grant conditions and use funds strictly as outlined in the proposal.

5. Reporting and Compliance:
- Maintain detailed records of expenditures and project progress.
- Prepare and submit periodic reports to grantors with

transparency and clarity.

6. AI Topic: Using AI to Find Grants:
- Explore AI-driven tools to streamline grant research and application processes.
- Maximize chances of securing funding by leveraging AI insights tailored to your business needs.

7. Conclusion:
- Embrace grants as a cornerstone of your business strategy for success and sustainability on Main Street.
- View the journey of grant procurement as an opportunity for growth and advancement in the business ecosystem of Hackensack.

OLD ******* CHAPTER 11 CRAFTING YOUR ONLINE

1. Creating a User-Friendly and Engaging Website:
- Choose a website platform (e.g., WordPress, Wix, Shopify) that suits your business needs.
- Design a layout with clear navigation and structured menus.
- Develop compelling content that reflects your brand identity and provides essential information.
- Enhance your website with high-quality visuals and ensure mobile responsiveness.

2. Basic Search Engine Optimization (SEO):
- Understand SEO principles and how they impact website visibility.
- Conduct keyword research using tools like Google Keyword Planner.
- Integrate keywords organically into your content, titles, and meta descriptions.

3. Leveraging Social Media for Brand Awareness:
- Identify the right social media platforms for your target audience.
- Create a content plan tailored to audience preferences and interests.

4. Online Advertising: Reach a Wider Audience:
- Utilize social media ads (e.g., Instagram, Facebook) to target specific demographics.
- Leverage Google Ads to connect with users actively seeking your products or services.

5. Managing and Updating Your Online Presence:
- Regularly update your website and social media profiles with the latest information.

- Monitor online reviews and engage with feedback to maintain a favorable brand reputation.

6. AI Topic: Leveraging AI and GenAI to Amplify Your Online Presence:
- Explore AI-driven website enhancement tools like Divi AI for personalized web design.
- Consider integrating AI chatbots to provide instant assistance and improve user experience.
- Utilize AI-powered SEO tools such as SEMRush, Yoast, MarketMuse, Clearscope, and Ahrefs' Content Explorer to optimize content and track performance.
- Harness AI-driven analytics to refine social media strategy and improve engagement.
- Implement AI in online advertising to target specific audiences and optimize ad spend.

7. Conclusion: Embracing AI for Growth:
- Consider incorporating AI into your online strategy to enhance customer connections, marketing efforts, and digital footprint.
- Embrace AI as a powerful ally that can help your business thrive in the digital age, freeing time to focus on core business activities.

CHAPTER 11 MASTERING OFFLINE MARKETING

1. Effective Use of Signage and Local Advertising:
- Choose strategic locations for signage to maximize visibility.
- Design signage with clear fonts, vibrant colors, and distinctive designs.
- Ensure signage communicates essential business details concisely.
- Explore grants and resources provided by local organizations for signage enhancement.

2. Hosting and Participating in Local Events:
- Research and identify local events aligned with your business offerings.
- Strategize interactive engagement tactics for event participation.
- Curate events that reflect your brand ethos and resonate with your target audience.
- Amplify event visibility through multichannel promotion.

3. Leveraging Local Media and Word of Mouth:
- Craft engaging press releases to garner attention from local publications.
- Participate in community-focused stories to amplify brand visibility.
- Exceed customer expectations to cultivate positive word-of-mouth endorsements.
- Implement loyalty programs and referral incentives to nurture customer loyalty.

4. Building Customer Loyalty Through Offline Channels:
- Develop loyalty initiatives that incentivize repeat patronage.

- Educate customers about loyalty benefits and seamlessly integrate promotion.
- Embrace personalized interactions to enhance customer satisfaction.

5. Using AI to Enhance Your Offline Strategy:
- Analyze customer data and local market trends to suggest effective offline marketing tactics.
- Measure the impact of offline marketing efforts using AI-generated insights.
- Make data-driven decisions to ensure offline marketing efforts are effective and efficiently targeted.

CHAPTER 12 ENGAGING YOUR COMMUNITY THROUGH EVENTS AND SPONSORSHIPS

1. Planning and Hosting Memorable Community Events:
- Identify the type of event that aligns with your business type and community interests.
- Organize event logistics, including scheduling, layout, staffing, and budgeting.
- Promote the event through multichannel strategies to maximize visibility.

2. Collaborating on Local Sponsorships:
- Research local opportunities that align with your business values and customer base.
- Evaluate sponsorship fit and negotiate for prominent branding placements.
- Foster meaningful interactions with event attendees through engaging promotional materials.

3. Running Successful Workshops and Classes:
- Develop workshop topics that showcase your business's expertise and resonate with your audience.
- Plan comprehensive session outlines and promotional materials for seamless execution.
- Leverage physical and digital channels to promote workshops and maximize attendee engagement effectively.

4. Leveraging Event Participation for Marketing:
- Research and choose events aligned with your target audience's interests and demographics.
- Curate inviting booth spaces that reflect your brand identity and encourage interaction.
- Capitalize on event momentum by nurturing post-

event relationships through personalized follow-up communications.

5. Measuring Success and Learning from Each Event:
- Gather feedback from attendees through surveys or informal conversations to gauge event satisfaction.
- Review event outcomes against predetermined objectives and refine strategies based on performance insights.
- Incorporate lessons from event evaluations to optimize future event planning and execution.

6. Using AI to Help with Events:
- Utilize AI to analyze local demographics, interests, and event attendance history to suggest themes likely to attract a large audience.
- Optimize event marketing using AI to identify the best channels and times for promotion.
- Evaluate event success post-event using AI-driven analysis to provide insights for future event planning.

CHAPTER 13 CUSTOMER SERVICE EXCELLENCE ON MAIN STREET

1. Understanding the Importance of Customer Service:
- Develop a customer-first philosophy.
- Identify the unique needs and expectations of the Hackensack community.

2. Training Your Team for Service Excellence:
- Conduct regular training sessions on communication, product knowledge, and conflict resolution.
- Foster a positive work environment to motivate and empower your team.

3. Creating a Customer Friendly Atmosphere:
- Design a welcoming physical environment that reflects your brand identity.
- Instill a culture of hospitality among your staff through warm greetings and proactive assistance.

4. Implementing Effective Feedback Mechanisms:
- Set up multiple feedback channels for customers to share their experiences.
- Actively seek feedback from customers to refine and improve your service.

5. Handling Complaints and Service Recovery:
- Establish clear protocols for addressing complaints and resolving issues promptly.
- Empower your employees to address complaints on the spot with autonomy and accountability.

6. Going Above and Beyond: Exceeding Expectations:
- Personalize the customer experience by tailoring services to individual preferences.

- Infuse unexpected gestures of appreciation into customer interactions to leave a lasting impression.

7. Leveraging Customer Service for Marketing:
- Cultivate a base of satisfied customers who advocate for your brand through word of mouth.
- Showcase stories of exceptional service through social media and marketing materials to bolster credibility.

8. Using AI to Transform Customer Service:
- Implement AI-enabled virtual assistants and chatbots to provide around-the-clock customer support.
- Analyze customer feedback using AI tools to identify common issues and trends for proactive improvement.

CHAPTER 14 SOCIAL MEDIA MARKETING

1. Choosing the Right Platforms for Your Business:
- Platforms like Facebook, Instagram, Twitter, LinkedIn, TikTok, and Pinterest cater to different demographics and purposes.
- Choose platforms based on your target audience and business objectives.

2. Creating Engaging Content Strategies:
- Understand your audience to create content that resonates with them.
- Utilize visuals, storytelling, trends, educational content, and interactive posts to engage your audience.
- Maintain a consistent posting schedule and diversify your content types.

3. Measuring and Analyzing Social Media Impact:
- Monitor engagement metrics, follower growth, website traffic, and conversion rates to gauge the effectiveness of your social media efforts.

4. Using AI in Social Media for Small Business:
- AI can assist in analyzing data, understanding your audience, and automating tasks like customer interactions, making social media marketing more efficient and effective.

5. Conclusion:
- Social media marketing is about connecting, engaging, and growing your business.
- Tell your story, build your community, and watch your business soar by leveraging the power of social media platforms and AI tools.

CHAPTER 15 MOBILE MARKETING ON MAIN STREET USA:

1. Online Visibility Check:
- Ensure your business ranks well in online searches, especially on platforms like Google Maps.
- Use the Profile Strength Indicator on Google to optimize your business profile.

2. Directory Listings:
- Invest in directory sites like Yelp, TripAdvisor, Nextdoor for Business, and the Yellow Pages.
- Update and optimize your business listings on these platforms to attract more customers.

3. Consider Mobile Apps:
- Assess the feasibility and cost-effectiveness of creating a standalone mobile app for your community.
- Evaluate the challenges of promoting and maintaining the app before deciding to proceed.

4. Explore Distrx:
- Download the Distrx app and search for your community to see if it's listed.
- Claim your business listing on Distrx and start promoting your business.
- Explore paid options for activities like walking tours and scavenger hunts to further engage with customers.

5. Continuously Monitor and Improve:
- Regularly monitor your online presence and engagement metrics.
- Seek customer feedback and make necessary adjustments to your mobile marketing strategies.

CHAPTER 16 REACHING THE NEW RESIDENTS

1. Identifying New Residents:
- Partner with real estate agents to reach out to new residents.
- Monitor social media for mentions of new moves and engage with newcomers.
- Offer referral benefits to existing customers to bring in new residents.

2. Hosting Community Welcome Events:
- Organize meet and greets or participate in community events to welcome new residents.
- Collaborate with local businesses and organizations to create a support network.

3. Utilizing Social Media:
- Post welcome messages and showcase community involvement on social media.
- Create content like local guides and settling-in tips to resonate with newcomers.

4. Engaging with Local Community Groups:
- Be active in local community groups and online forums, offering helpful advice without overt selling.
- Engage in casual conversations with new customers to gather feedback and build relationships.

CHAPTER 17: LEVERAGING AI IN SMALL BUSINESS MARKETING

1. Understanding AI in Marketing:
- Recognize AI as a pivotal tool in reshaping marketing strategy.
- Understand AI's transformative power in processing and analyzing vast data.

2. Addressing Local Marketing Challenges with AI:
- Utilize AI tools to attract new customers by analyzing geolocation data and social media trends.
- Enhance social media presence through AI-driven analytics and optimization.

3. AI Tools for Marketing:
- Explore various AI tools such as ChatGPT, Jasper, Lavender.ai, Canva, HubSpot, Hootsuite, and SEMrush.
- Understand the practical applications of AI across different business types.

4. Implementing AI Strategies:
- Personalize marketing efforts using AI insights to analyze customer data.
- Utilize AI for social media strategy by understanding audience interests and engagement patterns.

5. Ethical and Legal Considerations:
- Establish strict data privacy and security protocols to comply with regulations like GDPR and CCPA.
- Regularly audit AI algorithms to avoid biases and maintain fairness.

6. Staying Informed and Adaptable:
- Stay informed about new AI technologies and techniques for using AI in marketing.
- Develop flexible marketing strategies to incorporate new AI technologies as they emerge.

7. Integrating AI with Traditional Marketing Content:
- Blend AI insights with traditional marketing intuition for a balanced marketing strategy.
- Retain the human element in customer relationships and brand storytelling while leveraging AI for data-driven decisions.

8. GenAI Content Creation:
- Use AI tools like ChatGPT for content generation while ensuring content remains helpful and relevant to readers.
- Understand the evolving landscape of AI in marketing and continuously adapt strategies to remain competitive.

CHAPTER 18: SUSTAINING BUSINESS GROWTH AND INNOVATION

1. Cultivating Innovation:
- Hold regular innovation sessions to brainstorm and refine ideas.
- Encourage a culture where all ideas are welcomed and explored without fear of criticism.

2. Lifelong Learning as Your Business's Backbone:
- Foster a culture of continuous learning within your company.
- Develop tailored learning journeys for team members to align personal growth with business needs.
- Facilitate weekly wisdom exchanges where team members share new learnings and insights.

3. Smart Growth Strategies:
- Conduct readiness checks before implementing growth strategies to ensure preparedness.
- Stay true to the essence of your small business as you grow, maintaining personal touches and community engagement.

4. Conclusion:
- Sustain your growth by fostering a culture of innovation, continuous learning, and smart growth strategies.
- Keep pushing boundaries, embracing creativity, and never settling for "good enough."
- Embrace the motto "Forward Always," leveraging momentum for continued success.

CHAPTER 19: DEEPENING YOUR SMALL BUSINESS'S COMMUNITY CONNECTIONS

1. Embracing the B4 Strategy: Building Bonds Beyond Business
- Actively participate in community events and initiatives.
- Forge meaningful partnerships with local nonprofits, schools, and businesses.

2. Championing Sustainability and Social Responsibility
- Implement sustainable practices within your business operations.
- Give back to the community through various initiatives and donations.

3. Harnessing Technology for Community Engagement
- Support community-centric apps and platforms for local engagement.
- Utilize data analytics to understand community needs and tailor offerings accordingly.

4. Conclusion:
- Prioritize meaningful connections within your community for sustainable growth.
- Foster creativity and genuine engagement in your interactions.
- Utilize technology as a tool for community service and purpose-driven impact.

RESOURCE DIRECTORY

This Resource Directory offers a broad spectrum of tools, platforms, and services to cater to the diverse needs of small business owners, ranging from market research and branding to financial management and professional development. I've tried to be as comprehensive as possible, but I'm sure there is more to support your marketing and business growth efforts. Let me know if I've missed any!

CHAPTER 1: UNDERSTANDING YOUR MARKET

1. US Census Data:

- Website: [census. gov](https://www.census.gov/)
- Description: Access detailed demographic information, including age, gender, income, and household makeup of the Hackensack community.

2. Main Street Business Association (MSBA):

- Description: Offers substantial resources for compiling demographic data tailored to your business needs and assistance in market research.
- Contact: [Main Street Business Association](https://www.examplemsba.com)

3. Downtown Hackensack App:

- Website: www.linktr.ee/hackensack
- Description: Enhance visibility and accessibility for

locals and newcomers by listing your business on the Downtown Hackensack app developed with Distrx.

4. Local Gyms:

- Description: Consider collaborating with local gyms such as Kaizen Fitness or Femme for events or workshops related to health and wellness trends.

5. Apartment Complexes:

- Description: Collaborate with apartment complexes to promote exclusive deals for new residents, leveraging platforms like the Downtown Hackensack app.

6. Artificial Intelligence (AI) for Predictive Analytics:

- Description: Utilize AI tools for predictive analytics to stay ahead of customer preferences, trends, and local events.
- Example: Use AI-driven insights to tailor your café menu based on weather forecasts and social media trends.

7. Case Studies:

- Café Tranquilo: Learn from Café Tranquilo's success in attracting younger customers through menu revamping and Instagram marketing.
- TechTown Gadgets: Explore how TechTown Gadgets increased customer engagement by hosting tech workshops for residents.

CHAPTER 2: BRANDING YOUR BUSINESS

1. **Logo Design Services**:
   - Description: Professional logo design services can help conceptualize and create logos that represent your brand effectively.
   - Recommended Providers: Consider platforms like 99designs, Fiverr, or Upwork for freelance designers.

2. **Color Psychology Resources**:
   - Description: Explore resources on color psychology to understand how different colors evoke emotions and associations, aiding in choosing an effective color scheme for your brand.
   - Recommended Reading: "Color Psychology and Color Therapy" by Faber Birren.

3. **Brand Analysis and Development Tools**:
   - Description: AI-driven tools can provide insights into branding strategies, competitor analysis, and customer responses to marketing campaigns.
   - Recommended Tools: Look into AI platforms like Brandwatch, Sprout Social, or IBM Watson for AI-driven brand analysis.

4. **Customer Survey and Feedback Tools**:
   - Description: Collect customer feedback to assess brand perception and identify areas for improvement.

- Recommended Tools: To gather customer feedback, consider using survey platforms like SurveyMonkey, Google Forms, or Typeform.

5. **Brand Audit Checklist**:
- Description: Use a brand audit checklist to periodically review your brand identity and ensure alignment with business goals and customer expectations.
- Example Checklist: Develop a customized brand audit checklist tailored to your business needs, including logo evaluation, messaging consistency, and customer touchpoint analysis.

6. **Local Event Sponsorship Opportunities**:
- Description: Participate in or sponsor local events to engage with the community and reinforce your brand presence.
- Local Resources: Connect with organizations like Hackensack Cultural Center or local business associations to explore sponsorship opportunities.

7. **Collaboration Platforms for Local Businesses**:
- Description: Partner with other local businesses or artists to create unique products or experiences that reflect Hackensack's culture and community.
- Recommended Platforms: Consider using collaboration platforms like Slack or Trello to connect with

potential partners and coordinate joint projects.

CHAPTER 3 DIGITAL MARKETING ESSENTIALS FOR SMALL BUSINESSES

1. **Website Development and Local SEO**:
- Platforms: Use Shopify for easy e-commerce setup or WordPress for customizable websites.
- Local SEO: Register on Google My Business, incorporate local keywords, and encourage customer reviews.

2. **Content Marketing**:
- Blogging: Share insights, industry trends, and stories about your business on your website.
- Visual Content: Utilize Instagram and Pinterest to showcase appealing visuals related to your products or services.

3. **Social Media Engagement**:
- Platform Selection: Choose platforms where your target audience is active and engage regularly.
- Interaction: Respond to comments, run social media campaigns, and share behind-the-scenes glimpses of your business.

4. **Influencer Marketing**:
- Research: Choose influencers whose audience aligns with your target market and who demonstrate

authenticity.

- Budgeting: Be clear about your budget and expectations, and consider short-term partnerships for testing.

    5. **Email Marketing**:
- Platforms: Use Constant Contact or MailChimp to build and manage your email list.
- Personalization: Craft personalized newsletters with relevant content and offers for increased engagement.

    6. **AI-driven Marketing Tools**:
- Lavender.ai: Utilize AI tools like Lavender.ai to improve email marketing effectiveness and personalization

    7. **Hackensack Main Street Business Alliance** (DowntownHackensack.org): Support for businesses in Hackensack.

    8. **New Jersey Small Business Development** Centers (njsbdc.com): Business counseling and training.

    9. **Greater Bergen Community Action** (greaterbergen.org): Economic stability and business development resources.

CHAPTER 4: LOCAL OUTREACH AND NETWORKING

    1. **Community Engagement**:

- Get involved in local events and support community causes to build brand awareness and create positive associations with your business.

2. **Making the Most of Local Events**:
- Participate in and host events that reflect your business's personality and connect with your audience, leveraging opportunities to showcase your offerings.

3. **Strategic Collaborations with Other Businesses**:
- Identify complementary businesses for joint promotions and events, amplifying marketing efforts and expanding customer reach.

4. **Utilizing Local Media**:
- Use press releases, local advertising, and community features to effectively reach the Hackensack community by sharing news and stories about your business.

5. **Networking for Business Growth**:
- Join business networking groups, workshops, and seminars to connect with other local entrepreneurs and professionals, fostering opportunities for collaboration and growth.

CHAPTER 5 CUSTOMER RELATIONSHIP MANAGEMENT FOR SMALL BUSINESS

1. **Understanding the Fundamentals of CRM**:

- Recognize the importance of CRM in fostering lasting connections with customers, especially in community-oriented places like Hackensack.

2. **Building a Robust Customer Database**:
- Gather and maintain essential customer information ethically and transparently, ensuring you have the data to personalize interactions effectively.

3. **Enhancing the Customer Experience through Personalization**:
- Segment your customer base and tailor your communication and offers accordingly, making each customer feel valued and understood.

4. **Implementing Effective Loyalty Programs**:
- Design simple yet enticing loyalty programs to encourage repeat business and deepen customer loyalty, promoting them actively to ensure awareness.

5. **Utilizing CRM Tools for Analytics and Insights**:
- Choose the right CRM tool for your business and leverage data-driven insights to make informed decisions about marketing, service improvements, and product development.

6. **Using AI to Build Customer Loyalty**:
- Harness the power of AI to enhance customer loyalty programs by offering personalized rewards and

predicting customer behavior, thereby making each customer feel special and valued.

CHAPTER 6 ANALYTICS AND MEASURING SUCCESS

1. **Understanding the Value of Community Engagement**:

- Recognize the significance of going beyond mere business transactions to participate in and contribute to the community's welfare actively.
- Engage in local events and support community causes to demonstrate your commitment to the community's wellbeing, not just profit.

2. **Making the Most of Local Events**:

- Take advantage of the abundance of local events in Hackensack to connect with the community.
- Participate in events like street fairs and festivals or host events tailored to reflect your business's personality and resonate with your audience.

3. **Strategic Collaborations with Other Businesses**:

- Collaborate with complementary businesses to create joint promotions or events that benefit both parties.
- Identify potential partners and explore opportunities for cross-promotions, joint loyalty programs, or cohosted events to expand your reach.

4. **Utilizing Local Media**:

- Reach Hackensack residents through traditional local media outlets such as newspapers, blogs, and community podcasts.

- Share news about your business through press releases and local advertising, and consider participating in community features to enhance your visibility.

5. **Networking for Business Growth**:

- Build a network with fellow business owners and professionals in Hackensack through events like meetups and seminars.

- Joining business networking groups and the Chamber of Commerce can provide valuable opportunities for collaboration and growth.

6. **Using AI to Optimize Local Event Participation**:

- Employ AI to analyze community engagement patterns and preferences, helping you identify the most impactful events for your business.

- Personalize marketing strategies for these events to maximize engagement and refine future approaches based on feedback and social media engagement.

CHAPTER 7: BUDGETING AND RESOURCE ALLOCATION FOR SMALL BUSINESSES ON MAIN STREET

1. **Crafting a Realistic Marketing Budget**:
   - Establishing a structured marketing budget is crucial for small businesses.
   - Utilize a simple spreadsheet to track expenses and measure the effectiveness of marketing efforts.

2. **Percentage of Revenue Approach**:
   - Allocate a percentage of total revenue, typically 5-10%, for marketing activities.
   - This approach ensures that marketing efforts are proportionate to business size and revenue.

3. **Prioritizing Marketing Activities**:
   - Prioritize marketing expenditures based on potential return on investment.
   - Tailor marketing strategies to align with business objectives and target audience preferences.

4. **Maximizing Impact with Limited Resources**:
   - Explore cost-effective digital tools such as social media, email marketing, and basic SEO techniques.
   - Engage in community-based marketing initiatives like local events and networking to leverage grassroots support.

5. **Navigating the Costs of Digital Marketing**:
   - Allocate funds for online advertising, including social media campaigns and Google AdWords, while

setting realistic objectives and tracking ROI.

- Budget for website maintenance and SEO strategies, considering expenses like hosting and design fees.

6. **Balancing Short-term and Long-term Investments**:

- Distinguish between short-term tactics like seasonal promotions and long-term strategies such as brand cultivation and SEO efforts.

- Allocate a portion of the budget for sustained growth and long-term market presence.

7. **Tracking and Adjusting Your Marketing Budget**:

- Implement systems to monitor marketing expenses and evaluate their outcomes regularly.

- Remain flexible and adapt the budget in response to changing market dynamics and emerging opportunities.

8. **Budgeting Success Stories in Hackensack**:

- Draw inspiration from local businesses like Bistro Bonanza and Gadget Central, which achieved success through strategic budget allocation and marketing initiatives.

9. **AI Integration for Budget Optimization:**

- Harness AI tools to optimize resource allocation

and budgeting practices.

- AI can predict product demand, suggest optimal promotional campaign times, and provide insights into customer spending patterns.

- By leveraging AI-driven insights, businesses can tailor their marketing efforts and inventory management for maximum effectiveness and efficiency.

CHAPTER 8: STRATEGIC PARTNERSHIPS AND COLLABORATIONS

1. **Meetup**(meetup.com): Local networking groups and events.
2. **LinkedIn**(linkedin.com): Professional networking.
3. **BNI**(bni.com): Business networking organization.
4. **Alignable**(alignable.com): Networking tool for local businesses.

CHAPTER 9: IMPLEMENTING FUTURE MARKETING TRENDS FOR SMALL BUSINESS

1. **MarketingProfs**(marketingprofs.com): Marketing education and resources.
2. **Adweek**(adweek.com): Marketing and advertising news.
3. **Smart Insights** (smartinsights.com): Digital marketing advice.
4. **Content Marketing Institute** (contentmarketinginstitute.com): Content marketing strategy.

CHAPTER 10: GRANTS AND FUNDING OPPORTUNITIES FOR BUSINESSES

1. **Grants.gov**(grants.gov): Central location for federal grants.
2. **Small Business Administration** Grants

(sba.gov/fundingprograms/grants): Government grants for small businesses.
3. **Foundation Center** (foundationcenter.org): Directory of grantmaking foundations.

CHAPTER 11: MASTERING OFFLINE MARKETING

1. **Coursera** (coursera.org): Online courses in business and marketing.
2. **Udemy** (udemy.com): Courses on business skills.
3. **General Assembly** (generalassemb.ly): Training in digital marketing and business skills.

CHAPTER 12: ENGAGING YOUR COMMUNITY THROUGH EVENTS AND SPONSORSHIPS

1. **LegalZoom** (legalzoom.com): Online legal services.
2. **Nolo** (nolo.com): DIY legal books and software.
3. **U.S. Small Business Administration** Legal Requirements (sba.gov/businessguide/manageyourbusiness/legalrequirements): Guides for legal requirements.

CHAPTER 13: CUSTOMER SERVICE EXCELLENCE ON MAIN STREET

1. **Green Business Bureau**(greenbusinessbureau.com): Ecofriendly practices for businesses.
2. **EPA's Sustainable Marketplace** (epa.gov/greenerproducts): Environmentally preferable purchasing.
3. **Green America's Green Business Network** (greenamerica.org/greenbusinessnetwork) : Support for ecofriendly businesses.

CHAPTER 14: SOCIAL MEDIA MARKETING

1. **Social Media Platforms:**
   - **Facebook Business:** facebook.com/business

For creating business pages, advertising, and engaging with a broad audience.

- **Instagram for Business:** business.instagram.com

It focuses on visual content and storytelling and is ideal for reaching younger demographics.

- **Twitter for Business:** business.twitter.com

This is for real-time engagement, quick updates, and reaching a wide range of age groups.

- **LinkedIn Business:** linkedin.com/business

Best for B2B networking and professional content sharing.

- TikTok for Business: tiktok.com/business

For engaging with Gen Z and younger Millennials through creative short-form videos.

- **Pinterest Business:** business.pinterest.com

It is ideal for businesses with visually appealing products targeting primarily female demographics.

2. **Content Creation Tools:**

- **Canva:** canva.com

User-friendly graphic design tool for creating social media graphics, posters, and more.

- **Adobe Spark:** spark.adobe.com

Offers tools for creating graphics, web pages, and video stories.

- **Unsplash:** unsplash.com

Free high-resolution photos for enhancing social media posts.

- **Lumen5:** lumen5.com

Converts blog posts into engaging videos, useful for content repurposing.

3. **Scheduling and Management Tools:**

- **Hootsuite:** hootsuite.com

They monitor social media traffic and campaign management for scheduling posts.

- **Buffer:** buffer.com

Simplifies social media posting and provides analytics.

- **Later:** later.com

Visual content calendar and scheduling tool, especially useful for Instagram.

- **Sprout Social:** sproutsocial.com

Comprehensive tool for planning, publishing, engagement, and analytics.

4. **Analytics and Reporting Tools:**

- **Google Analytics:** analytics.google.com

It tracks website traffic and user behavior from social media sources.

- **Facebook Insights and Instagram Analytics**: These are integrated within the platforms and provide in-depth insights into audience engagement and performance.
- **Twitter Analytics:** analytics.twitter.com

This is for tracking tweet performance, audience demographics, and engagement.

- **SocialBakers**: socialbakers.com

AI-powered marketing suite for analyzing social media performance.

5. Educational Resources:

- **HubSpot Academy:** academy.hubspot.com

Offers free online training in social media strategy and content marketing.

- **Social Media Examiner:** socialmediaexaminer.com

Provides insights, tips, and trends on social media marketing.

- **Hootsuite Academy:** education.hootsuite.com

Offers courses and certifications in social media marketing.

CHAPTER 15: MOBILE MARKETING ON MAIN STREET USA

1. **Google Maps:**
- Maintain accurate business information on Google Maps.
- Utilize the Profile Strength Indicator for completeness.
- Take control of your online presence easily.

2. **Directory Sites:**
- Explore platforms like Yelp, Tripadvisor, Nextdoor for Business, and Yellow Pages.
- Leverage directory listings and reviews for increased visibility.
- Consider paid advertising and promotion options for maximum impact.

3. **Mobile Apps:**
- Evaluate the necessity and feasibility of creating a standalone mobile app for your community.
- Recognize the challenges of promoting and distributing a community-specific app.
- Consider alternative solutions like Distrx, a location-aware mobile app for marketing communities and small businesses.
- Utilize Distrx's features such as community map, business directory, event calendar, and promotional opportunities.
- Claim your business listing, promote, and engage with the

Distrx app for free.

CHAPTER 16: REACHING THE NEW RESIDENTS

1. **Identifying New Residents:**
- Partner with Real Estate Agents: Collaborate with local brokers and property managers to introduce new residents to community resources.
- Social Media Monitoring: Monitor local social media groups for mentions of new moves and engage with welcoming messages.
- Referral Benefits: Incentivize existing customers to refer new residents to your business through discounts or rewards.

2. **Hosting Community Welcome Events:**
- Organize Meet-and-Greets: Host informal events in your store to welcome new residents and foster connections with local businesses.
- Participate in Community Events: Increase visibility by engaging with newcomers by participating in community events and festivals.

3. **Collaborating with Local Businesses and Organizations:**
- Foster partnerships with fellow local businesses for cross-promotions and collaborative events to support new residents.

4. **Utilizing Social Media for Local Engagement:**
- Share welcome messages and showcase community involvement to attract and engage new residents on social media platforms.
- Create Content That Resonates: Develop content such as local guides and settling-in tips to provide valuable information to newcomers.

5. **Engaging with Local Community Groups and Forums:**
- Participate actively in local community groups and forums to answer questions and provide helpful advice, building credibility and relationships.

6. **Feedback Loop with New Customers:**
- Initiate casual conversations with new residents to gather feedback and insights into their needs and experiences, fostering stronger relationships.

CHAPTER 17: LEVERAGING AI IN SMALL BUSINESS MARKETING

1. **AI Tools for Marketing:**
- ChatGPT for Content Creation: Utilize ChatGPT for drafting emails, blog posts, video scripts, and generating marketing campaign ideas.
- Jasper for Content Creation: Jasper provides content ideas and sample sentences to help generate marketing copy, blog posts, and social media content.

- Lavender.ai for Email Optimization: Use Lavender.ai to analyze and improve sales and marketing emails for better engagement and effectiveness.
- Canva's AI-Enhanced Design: Leverage Canva's AI suggestions for layouts, color palettes, and branding elements to create visually appealing designs.

2. **Practical Applications Across Business Types:**
- Cafés and Restaurants: Personalize marketing efforts, menu adjustments, and reservation systems with AI insights.
- Tech Shops: Predict trends, enhance recommendations, and automate after-sales service communications using AI.
- Legal Firms: Streamline scheduling, client relationship management, and market positioning with AI.
- Nail Salons and Barber Shops: Efficiently schedule appointments, analyze trends, and create targeted advertising campaigns with AI tools.

3. **Implementing AI in Marketing Operations:**
- Personalized Marketing with AI: Collect customer data, segment customers, and create tailored marketing campaigns based on AI insights.
- AI for Social Media Strategy: Use AI analytics to understand audience behavior, optimize content, and measure campaign performance.

4. **Understanding AI Mechanics:**

- **Machines Learning from Data:** Understand how machines use algorithms to learn from data, identify patterns, and make decisions.
- **Natural Language Processing:** Explore how AI understands and generates human-like text for content creation and customer service.

5. **Ethical and Legal Considerations:**
- **Data Privacy and Security:** Establish strict protocols for data privacy and security to comply with regulations like GDPR and CCPA.
- **Transparency and Bias Mitigation:** Regularly audit AI algorithms to ensure fairness, avoid biases, and maintain customer transparency.

6. **Continuous Learning and Adaptation:**
- **Stay Informed:** Learn about new AI technologies and techniques through blogs, podcasts, and continuous learning.
- **Flexibility in Strategy:** Develop marketing strategies that can adapt to incorporate new AI technologies as they emerge, investing in AI solutions to enhance efficiency and effectiveness.

CHAPTER 18: SUSTAINING BUSINESS GROWTH AND INNOVATION

1. **Cultivating Innovation:**

- Innovation Sessions: Host creativity boot camps where team members and outsiders can share and refine ideas without judgment, encouraging a culture of innovation.
- Lifelong Learning: Foster a culture of continuous learning within the company by developing tailored learning plans for team members and organizing weekly wisdom exchanges.

2. **Smart Growth Strategies:**
- Readiness Check: Before implementing growth strategies, assess the business's capacity to handle growth regarding systems, team readiness, and scalability.
- Staying True to Your Roots: While expanding, maintain the essence of the small business, including personal touches, a community feel, and genuine care for customers.

CHAPTER 19: DEEPENING YOUR SMALL BUSINESS'S COMMUNITY CONNECTIONS

1. **Embracing the B4 Strategy: Building Bonds Beyond Business:**
- Active Community Engagement: Participate in community events, sponsor local initiatives, and organize activities that benefit the community.
- Meaningful Partnerships: Collaborate with local nonprofits, schools, and businesses on projects and events that align with your values and resonate with the community.

2. **Championing Sustainability and Social Responsibility:**
- Sustainable Practices: Implement environmentally friendly practices in your business operations and share your journey with the community to inspire others.
- Giving Back: Find creative ways to give back to the community, such as offering space for gatherings, mentoring youth, or donating proceeds to charitable causes.

3. **Harnessing Technology for Community Engagement:**
- Community Apps: Utilize community-centric apps to promote local engagement, share updates, and showcase exclusive deals, fostering a sense of unity.
- Data-Driven Insights: Use data analytics to understand community needs and preferences, collaborating with local improvement districts for valuable insights.

RESOURCE DIRECTORY FOR AI / GENERATIVE AI (GENAI)

1. Chat GPT

Website: https://openai.com/chatgpt

Description: Chat GPT is an advanced AI language model developed by OpenAI. It can understand and generate humanlike text, making it useful for content creation, customer service, and more.

2. Jasper

Website: https://www.jasper.ai/

Description: Jasper is an AI-powered content platform that assists in creating engaging marketing copy. It is designed to help overcome writer's block and generate ideas for various content types.

3. Claude AI

Website: https://claude.ai

Description: This ChatGPT competitor is picking up some significant speed at the time of this writing. Whether they can catch ChatGPT is unknown. Claude can read up to 75,000 words, say a book fairly quickly, and answer any questions about it. The major difference between ChatGPT and Claude is how the LLMs (large language models) were trained. But that topic is very deep and not for this book.

4. Canva

Website: https://www.canva.com

Description: Canva is a user-friendly graphic design tool that integrates AI to suggest layouts, color palettes, and branding elements, aiding businesses in creating visually appealing marketing materials.

5. HubSpot

Website: https://www.hubspot.com/

Description: HubSpot provides a comprehensive CRM and marketing automation platform enhanced with AI capabilities. It's suitable for managing customer relationships, automating marketing tasks, and gaining insights from data.

6. Hootsuite

Website: https://www.hootsuite.com/

Description: Hootsuite is a social media management tool that incorporates AI to streamline the process of scheduling posts, managing engagement, and analyzing social media campaign performance.

7. SEMrush

Website: https://www.semrush.com/

Description: SEMrush is an online visibility management and content marketing platform that offers AI-driven SEO insights. It helps businesses improve their search engine optimization and online presence.

8. Lavender.ai

Website: https://www.lavender.ai

Description: Lavender analyzes your sales and marketing emails to see what's working and then provides feedback so you can make changes to improve your communications.

9. Upmetrics

Website: https://upmetrics.co/

Description: Perfect for small businesses, Upmetrics allows you to build your business plan with its AI-powered platform. They have hundreds of business plan templates.

10. Sniper AI

Website: https://sniperai.com

Description: Their HR management tools are good for small business HR automation. It also includes many other tools that allow you to handle everything from candidate tracking to hiring to onboarding.

11. You.com

Website: https://you.com

Description: You.com claims to be a personalized version of AI. If you sign up for PRO at $15/month (annual), you get a customized front-end user interface for a few AI tools. I've just started using it, and I like it.

There's no one-size-fits-all.

Before signing up for paid accounts, you should explore these to understand how they can best serve your business needs.

ABOUT THE AUTHOR

John T. Peters is the award-winning serial entrepreneur and digital innovator who leads the Main Street Business Alliance and Downtown Hackensack's Special Improvement District with 160 commercial properties and 375 small businesses. He's also the former President of the Travel Media Group at USA Today/Gannett, showcasing his prowess in luxury travel, hospitality, and media. John's strategic vision and digital expertise have driven two startups to successful acquisitions and led growth initiatives for large public companies, increasing revenues to $360M. John excels in the dynamic business environment and is adept at embracing challenges and creating big-picture opportunities. His marketing, business development, and digital savviness, gained from leading roles at top companies, make him an industry authority and sought-after speaker. Featured in The New York Times, USA TODAY, Reuters, US News, the LA Times, and many others, John's focus on customer experience and strategic partnerships highlights his innovative approach to business growth and digital transformation, including expansive use of Artificial Intelligence.